Michael Turback

111 Places in the Finger Lakes That You Must Not Miss

Photographs by Brian Wilder

111

emons:

For Ellie and Ben

Bibliographical information of the Deutsche Nationalbibliothek
The Deutsche Nationalbibliothek lists this publication in the Deutsche Nationalbibliografie; detailed bibliographical data are available on the internet at http://dnb.d-nb.de.

MIX
Paper | Supporting responsible forestry
FSC® C177064

Cäcilienstraße 48, 50667 Köln
info@emons-verlag.de

Layout: Eva Kraskes, based on a design
by Lübbeke | Naumann | Thoben
Maps: altancicek.design, www.altancicek.de
Basic cartographical information from Openstreetmap,
© OpenStreetMap-Mitwirkende, OdbL
Edited by: Ros Horton
Printing and binding: sourc-e GmbH
Printed in Europe 2025
ISBN 978-3-7408-2466-2
First edition

Guidebooks for Locals & Experienced Travellers
Join us in uncovering new places around the world at
www.111places.com

Foreword

There's no place on Earth quite like the Finger Lakes, and there's never been a book about the region quite like this one.

An exceptionally beautiful 4,692-square-mile corner of Upstate New York, the Finger Lakes are dotted with historic cities, vast farmland, vineyards, dramatic gorges, waterfalls and waterways. But perhaps most intriguing are the region's many eccentricities, beginning with Indigenous folklore. The earliest inhabitants believed the lakes were formed when the Great Spirit laid his hands on the land to bless it, and His fingers left imprints that filled with water.

Think of this book as an armchair field guide of sorts to the odd, the offbeat, the fascinating and mysterious, the just plain unexpected – a book that explores the region's often overlooked stories, legends, and best-kept secrets. It's filled with curious characters – religious zealots, daredevils, explorers, suffragettes, inventors, benefactors, artists and writers, winemakers and brewmasters, bootleggers and scoundrels.

Visit the birthplace of women's rights, the home of the first ice cream sundae, the world's fastest carousel, waterfalls taller than Niagara, a haunted winery, a brain collection, and a circus school. Drive over a bridge that inspired a classic movie. Search for a Gilded Age secret garden, a Gothic castle, a six-story treehouse, a life-sized *papier-mâché* dinosaur, and a faithful recreation of Monet's garden. Discover the drive-in that time forgot, a Confederate POW camp, an anarchist's flower shop, a tavern with an electric chair, Harriet Tubman's hometown, Mark Twain's gravesite, and find out what in the world Amelia Earhart was doing here.

When you put all these places and stories together, it's like lifting a curtain, and hardly surprising that the Finger Lakes has been called picturesque and enchanting, curious and creative, historic and inventive – it's all those things and more.

111 Places

CORTLAND CORSET COMPANY

1 Alex Haley Municipal Pool

Watery roots

The Greater Ithaca Activities Center (GIAC), a local center for youth and teens, serves the community by providing multicultural, educational, and recreational programs. The public pool is a key part of the center, a space for swimming and swimming lessons. Named for celebrated author Alex Haley, who was born just a few blocks away, the pool features a striking mural at the entrance, designed and painted in 2015 by the late Khalil Bey, its theme intended to celebrate the writer's achievements.

In 1921, Alex Haley's father, Simon Alexander Haley, was finishing his Master's degree in agriculture at Cornell University when his wife, Bertha Palmer Haley, who was studying at the Ithaca Conservatory of Music, gave birth to Alex. Less than two months later, the family moved to Tennessee, where Alex spent the early years of his life. Despite his brief time in Ithaca, the city has embraced its connection to Haley, author of works including *The Autobiography of Malcolm X*, *Queen*, and, of course, *Roots: The Saga of an American Family.*

Roots was based on his own family history, dating back to the year 1767. The story of Kunta Kinte's descendants would not only secure the author's place as an important voice in Black history, but also allow Americans to visualize the African American cultural journey. More than half the US population watched *Roots* when it was adapted for television.

Haley's image anchors the narrative of the mural, highlighting his significant contributions to literature and African American history. Children holding hands represent the diversity and collective spirit of the Ithaca community. Sketches of the author's books are accompanied by the message: "Go to the Library," and the artist asks in painted letters, "When did you first hear about Alex Haley? Did you know he wrote books? Did you know he was born right here? His house is right down the street."

Address 408 North Albany Street, Ithaca, NY 14850, + 1 (607) 277-6169, www.cityofithaca.org | Getting there Follow Route 13 and 34 north, then right onto West Court Street and continue to the corner of North Albany Street | Hours Daily noon–8pm | Tip A memorial pocket park at the home where Haley was born features a silver maple tree on the property, a descendant of the tree that shaded his grandmother's porch in Tennessee, where she taught him about his African ancestry (212 Cascadilla Street, Ithaca, NY 14850, www.thehistorycenter.net).

2 Andy Goldsworthy Memorial

A human collaboration with nature

Cornell Botanic Gardens, the legacy of horticulturist and botanist Liberty Hyde Bailey, encompasses over 4,300 acres of natural areas, gardens, and arboreta, making it one of the largest university botanical gardens in America. It was in a tranquil part of the gardens called the F. R. Newman Arboretum where environmental artist Andy Goldsworthy chose to honor victims of the Holocaust.

Known for ephemeral works created outdoors from natural materials in collaboration with nature, in 2004, Goldsworthy began planning a stone garden inspired by the Jewish tradition of placing stones on graves when visiting a cemetery, rather than flowers, to symbolize lasting memory. Four granite boulders, on indefinite loan from the Museum of Jewish Heritage in New York City, were selected by the artist, in his words, "because of their violent history, first created in fires of the inner earth, then erupted through the ground, only to be moved and worn by crushing glacial ice." The boulders, each weighing between four and eight tons, were set in place by crane, and three were cored with a 4,000-degree blowtorch to accommodate a small irrigation system, soil, and young trees. On May 5, 2005, several Holocaust survivors planted three dwarf chestnut oaks, seen protruding from the rocks.

Goldsworthy's garden is intended to be visited and revisited, presenting new experiences as the garden matures over time. As the trees and boulders mature, visitors may see the boulders crack as the trunks thicken, and as the trees become firmly rooted in the ground, some will survive, while others may not.

Goldsworthy's work represents an interplay of natural materials and the natural environment, a reminder of the resilience of Jewish identity. The installation is an extension of the Garden of Stones by the artist at the Museum of Jewish Heritage, an 18-boulder version of his work.

Address 124 Comstock Knoll Drive, Ithaca, NY 14850, www.iaujc.org/goldsworthy-holocaust-memorial | Getting there Take Route 366 (Dryden Road) out of downtown Ithaca and follow the sign to the Botanic Gardens | Hours Daily 6am–6pm | Tip Another local Goldsworthy installation, an egg-shaped cairn of locally quarried Llenroc limestone, can be found along the Hoyt-Pileated Trail in the Sapsucker Woods Sanctuary, across from the Lab of Ornithology (159 Sapsucker Woods Road, Ithaca, NY 14850).

3 Arthur Dove Block

America's first abstract artist

Born in Canandaigua in 1880, Arthur Garfield Dove attended Hobart College in Geneva for two years, then enrolled at Cornell University in Ithaca. After graduation in 1903, he moved to New York City and worked as an illustrator for *Harper's Magazine* and *The Saturday Evening Post*. Later, with the encouragement of Alfred Stieglitz, photographer and art promoter, Dove began creating works inspired by natural forms, now regarded as the first purely abstract paintings by an American artist.

In 1933, he returned to Geneva, where for the next five years he painted over 100 abstract watercolors each year, the most productive period in his artistic career. The third floor of the Dove Block, a handsome brick building constructed by his father, William Dove, a successful brickmaker, became his residence and studio. (The words "Dove Block" are inscribed on a rectangular block centered in the cornice of the building's Exchange Street façade.)

The building now houses a community arts center called the Dove Block Project. The first floor features both rotating works from up-and-coming artists, as well as a small theater that screens a short film about Geneva during the time the artist lived and worked here. A long wall on the third floor, where Dove exhibited his most provocative work, is documented in a 1938 studio photo featured in the Smithsonian's Archives of American Art. When you visit, take the elevator to the third floor to see museum-grade reproductions of Dove's paintings arranged on that wall, exactly as captured in the historic photograph.

Arthur Dove's works are displayed in museums across New York City, Chicago, and Boston. The Phillips Collection in Washington, DC owns the largest number. In upstate New York, permanent collections of both Rochester's Memorial Art Gallery and the Herbert F. Johnson Museum of Art at Cornell include his paintings.

Address 465 Exchange Street, Geneva, NY 14456, +1 (315) 325-8160, www.thedoveblockproject.org | Getting there From Routes 5 & 20, take East Castle Street to the corner of Exchange Street | Hours Wed–Sun noon–4pm | Tip Over the years, Houghton House has been a private school, an inn, and a college dorm. Today it's home to the Art and Architecture Department of Hobart and William Smith Colleges, featuring works from the school's art collection (1 Kings Lane, Geneva, NY 14456, www.hws.edu).

4 The Auburn Doubledays

Behind every great mustache…

The baseball stadium was built in 1926 by the Polish Falcons, a local branch of a national Polish-American social organization. Its old wooden grandstand stood until 1995, when it was replaced with a 2,800-seat facility to comply with standards for minor league ballparks. As of 2004, the venue's full name is Leo Pinckney Field at Falcon Park, honoring the long-time sportswriter for *The Auburn Citizen* who was instrumental in bringing a professional sports franchise to his hometown.

Over the decades, scores of would-be Major League Baseball players have cut their pro-ball teeth on the weathered turf and well-worn bases at the Auburn ballpark, infamous throughout the league for its four-foot drop from home plate to center field. Today, the Auburn Doubledays of the New York-Penn League, an affiliate of the Washington Nationals, play their home games here every summer.

The team is named for Abner Doubleday, who spent his childhood in Auburn, then attended a private preparatory high school in Cooperstown. Legend has it that Doubleday invented the game of baseball, the evolution from a variety of stick-and-ball contests played at the time, with the first game allegedly played in Cooperstown on June 12, 1839.

Besides hosting the Doubledays, Falcon Park is also a gathering place for the community. In the 1950s, the setting was used as a speedway for kids who raced go-karts along a 10th-mile track around the infield. In other years, the stadium has presented a range of musical concerts, and the Auburn High School baseball team plays its home contests at the stadium.

When Falcon Park's spectator stands fill with families, they're entertained by the team's official mascot, costumed in a likeness of Abner Doubleday, rocking his signature mustache. The character provides Auburn with a team-generated slogan, "Our mascot has the best mustache in minor league baseball."

Address 130 North Division Street, Auburn, NY 13021, +1 (315) 255-2489, www.auburndoubledays.com | Getting there From Routes 5 & 20, turn onto North Division Street | Hours See website for home game schedule | Tip On October 18, 1928, Babe Ruth and Lou Gehrig made a stop in Elmira as part of their post-World Series barnstorming tour. In an exhibition game at Dunn Field, Ruth delivered a 500-foot home run over the left centerfield fence (546 Luce Street, Elmira, NY 14904, www.theelmirapioneers.com).

5 Auburn Prison

Going to work for Copper John

Not every city has a maximum security prison in the middle of downtown, especially one designed with castle-like turrets and battlements. One of the oldest and most historically significant correctional facilities in the United States, Auburn Prison received its first consignment of 53 prisoners in 1817.

During the 1880s, there was growing public concern about the inhumane nature of hangings, and it was believed that electrocution could provide a quicker and less painful death. Edwin F. Davis, an Auburn electrician, wired the first electric chair, and on August 6, 1890, William Kemmler, who had murdered his wife Tillie with a hatchet, became the first person sent to the chair. On September 6, 1901, while attending the Pan-American Exposition in Buffalo, President William McKinley was shot by Leon Czolgosz. After his conviction of first-degree murder, Czolgosz became the second occupant of Auburn's "hot seat," electrocuted by three jolts, 1,800 volts each, just six weeks after McKinley's death.

Overseeing its long history, Copper John has stood sentry over the city atop the prison walls, symbolically protecting citizens from the inmates. The statue of a Revolutionary War soldier "on duty" was placed atop the administration building while it was still under construction in the 1820s. The original figure was carved of wood, then replaced in 1848 by a replica, hammered out of sheet copper by inmates in the prison foundry. Being sentenced to the Auburn Correctional Facility is called "going to work for Copper John."

In 2004, the state learned that the statue was "anatomically correct," and ordered the statue to be "uncorrected." Prisoners mischievously protested the decision and campaigned to "Save Copper John's Johnson." No such luck. Look for Copper John, without the bulge in his crotch, towering above the roof of the main prison building facing State Street.

Address 135 State Street, Auburn, NY 13024, +1 (315) 253-8401 | **Getting there** From downtown Auburn, follow State Street (Route 38) to the corner of Wall Street | **Hours** Viewable from the outside only | **Tip** The prison put Auburn on the map, and Prison City Brewing put Auburn on the craft beer map. In a downtown building that once served as a Civil War-era armory, crowds now knock down pints of an IPA called Mass Riot (28 State Street, Auburn, NY 13021, www.prisoncitybrewing.com).

6 Barton Hall

The long, strange trip to Cornell

The date was May 8, 1977. Beginning that afternoon, 8,500 Deadheads crammed into the Cornell University gymnasium for a three-hour Grateful Dead show, one that ardent fans consider to be the greatest performance among their 2,300 concerts during the band's 30-year career.

Built in 1917 and originally called the New York State Armory and Drill Hall, Barton Hall was, at the time, the largest unpillared room in existence, covering almost two acres. It served as a ground school for military aeronautics during World War I, then as a drill deck and armory during World War II. It was home to the Cornell basketball team from 1919 to 1990 and also to the indoor track team from the 1920s to the present. In the days prior to online course registration, students registered for classes in Barton. As a concert venue, Barton Hall has hosted hundreds of performers, including Bob Dylan, The Rolling Stones, Bruce Springsteen, Elton John, and B. B. King. But that iconic '77 show will forever link Cornell and the Grateful Dead.

The band was brought to campus by the student-run Concert Commission. Advance tickets were priced at $6.50 each and sold for $7.50 on the day of the show. Fans came for the Dead's blend of folk, rock, blues, jazz, and country – an experimental, improvised style that made each live performance a unique experience. That day, the band's playing was tight and inspired, a total of 19 songs over two sets; and fueled by bootleg recordings circulated among fans, the band's Barton Hall show has achieved legendary status. In 2012, a recording of the performance was inducted into the Library of Congress' National Recording Registry.

Over the years, Deadheads from all parts of the world have visited Barton Hall to connect with the history and spirit of that day. They gather, share stories, and celebrate their love for the band's music.

Address 117 Statler Drive, Ithaca, NY 14853, +1 (607) 255-7775, www.cornellbigred.com/facilities/barton-hall | Getting there On central campus, follow Campus Road to Statler Drive | Hours Daily 9am–11pm | Tip One of Ithaca's most popular restaurants, Moosewood is home of the iconic vegetarian cookbook. When the Grateful Dead arrived in town, they had lunch at Moosewood, and despite the fact that the band was at the height of their fame, no one recognized them (215 North Cayuga Street, Ithaca, NY 14850, www.moosewoodrestaurant.com).

7 Biggest Pair of Pants

Not for the faint of waist

The charming village of Homer is basically a Hallmark movie. This place has tree-lined streets, homes with manicured lawns and gardens, a village green surrounded by old brick churches, and a quaint, picturesque downtown. Homer provided inspiration for "Homeville," the setting in the novel *David Harum: A Story of American Life* by Edward Noyes Westcott, a portrait of small-town life in America at the turn of the 20th century.

The Homer Men and Boys Store has been a cornerstone of the village since Roland "Frog" Fragnoli, an Italian immigrant, opened its doors in 1951. Specializing in durable, no-nonsense, workwear-inspired clothing, the store carries everyday essentials – no cocktail dresses or designer handbags here. Frog's motto was always, "If we don't have it, you don't need it." The store is now in the hands of Frog's daughter, Leslee Fragnoli Garrison, who upholds her father's legacy and remains committed to his values.

There's something timeless about this store. It's a hometown mainstay with the welcoming spirit of a place that tourists love to stumble upon. Folks still talk about the day comedian Bill Murray walked in to buy a "Homer" imprinted shirt for his son, whose name just happens to be Homer.

The store carries its own line of Homer-branded jeans, piled high on shelves, but the jeans everyone talks about are one extraordinary pair on the second floor. It seems that back in the mid-1980s, the Wrangler company held a "Guess the Stitches Contest," featuring an 8-foot-tall pair of its signature denim jeans, measuring from the floor to the ceiling, with a 64-inch waist, pockets, belt loops, and a Wrangler leather patch. Customers were invited to guess how many stitches it took to make the jeans, and the three closest guesses won a free pair of normal-size Wranglers. The "biggest pair of jeans" on display has been a tourist attraction ever since.

Address 11 South Main Street, Homer, NY 13077, +1 (607) 749-3314, www.homermenandboys.com | **Getting there** From Cortland, follow Route 11 for 3 miles (becomes South Main Street in Homer) | **Hours** Mon–Wed 8:30am–6pm, Thu & Fri 8:30am–7pm, Sat 8:30am–5pm | **Tip** It's a short walk to the birthplace of William Osborn Stoddard, who became Assistant Private Secretary to Abraham Lincoln. Stoddard personally wrote the first draft of the Emancipation Proclamation from the president's notes (5 Albany Street, Homer, NY 13077).

8 Birdsong Fairy Trail

Gnome homes of Mendon Pond

A quaint town in the northwest corner of the Finger Lakes region, Mendon is the home of a 2,500-acre park, once an ancient Native American hunting and fishing site and a camping ground for early French explorers. Present day Mendon Ponds Park is an extraordinary place, with unique geological features, a nature preserve, sensory garden, and nearly 30 miles of self-guided hiking trails, considered to be some of the best examples of surviving Indigenous trails in the region.

Best known and most popular of the wooded park trails, the Birdsong Fairy Trail features a series of enchanting attractions and unexpected surprises for outdoor explorers. Just steps away from the Wild Wings Nature Center, visitors discover a magical world of intricate little dwellings inhabited by fairies, each with their own unique design and personality.

Some of the diminutive abodes are discreetly tucked in a tree hollow or artfully incorporated into a root; others mounted on a stone or hanging from a tree branch. Some houses sit on a stump; others are part way up tree trunks. Many of the doors are painted into interesting tree features, a few are framed with horseshoes, and most have miniature door handles. There are tiny swings, a ladder of twigs, tree bridges, troll holes, and small signs. One sign is a quote from Roald Dahl, British author of children's literature: "Those who don't believe in magic will never find it."

Beginning in 2019, the structures started to pop up along this section of the park trails, the work of Chris Marshall, a school facilities director and amateur woodworker, and his wife Betsy Marshall, a school parent educator, who draw upon fairy-tale lore and a bit of pixie dust to create these small wonders. And while mystical creatures have inhabited the minds and imaginations of children for years, people of all ages delight in the magic they've created here.

Address 95 Douglas Road, Honeoye Falls, NY 14472, +1 (585) 753-7275, www.gofingerlakes.org/mendonponds | Getting there Take Thruway exit 11; follow Clover Road (Route 65) to Pond Road (Mendon Ponds West), or from Routes 5 & 20, follow Route 64 to Route 252 (Rush-Mendon Road), then right onto Route 65 to the Pond Road park entrance | Hours Daily 6am–11pm | Tip Mendon Ponds Park contains a number of unique glacially created oddities, including a "kettle" known as the "Devil's Bathtub," a roughly circular depression left behind by melting ice blocks. The sunken pond is a short hike down a staircase from the upper parking lot.

9 The Boating Museum

Whatever floats your boat

In the language of the native Iroquois, Keuka means "Canoe Landing," so it's not surprising to find the long and storied history of Finger Lakes boating being told right here in the Keuka Lake village of Hammondsport. Native Americans used canoes and other small craft for fishing and transportation before white settlers began building commercial vessels to transport goods to markets around the lakes and beyond.

With the demise of the one-time giant Taylor Wine Company, in 1996, the former production complex became available to a group of dedicated antique boat *aficionados* who worked with New York State's Department of Education to establish the Finger Lakes Boating Museum. Two floors of the main building are dedicated to exhibit spaces that display a growing collection, including canoes, rowboats, powerboats, sailboats, cruising boats, trout boats, outboard runabouts, hydroplanes, and luxury pleasure boats – more boats than you can shake an oar at – all built either by regional manufacturers or those with local ties.

One of the museum's on-loan treasures is the *Elizabeth Ellen*, a 26-foot special launch, built of cypress wood in 1910 by the Faye and Bowen Engine Company in Geneva. Lavishly restored in 2003 with leather-upholstered benches, wicker chairs, and an oriental carpet, it's on prominent display with a picnic basket inside, imagining its many past outings across the lake.

The Steamboat Room contains two dozen miniature, to-scale steamboats that became a vital part of transportation on the four major lakes for both passengers and cargo from the 1830s until the 1920s. There's a Motorboat Room, a Rowboat Hall, a Canoe Room, and an active Restoration Shop where volunteers regularly work on a variety of boats. A classroom offers lectures, workshops, and boat-safety programs, and a video theater shows a 13-minute film about the history of boating in the region.

Address 8231 Pleasant Valley Road, Hammondsport, NY 14840, +1 (607) 569-2222, www.flbm.org | **Getting there** Drive south on Route 54, turn onto South Valley Road, then right onto Pleasant Valley Road | **Hours** Daily 10am–5pm | **Tip** After learning everything you ever wanted to know about boats, book a 90-minute water excursion on Keuka Lake on the *Pat II*, a 39-foot tour boat, originally built in 1924, and restored at the Finger Lakes Boating Museum (7 Water Street, Hammondsport, NY 14840, pat2boat@flbm.org).

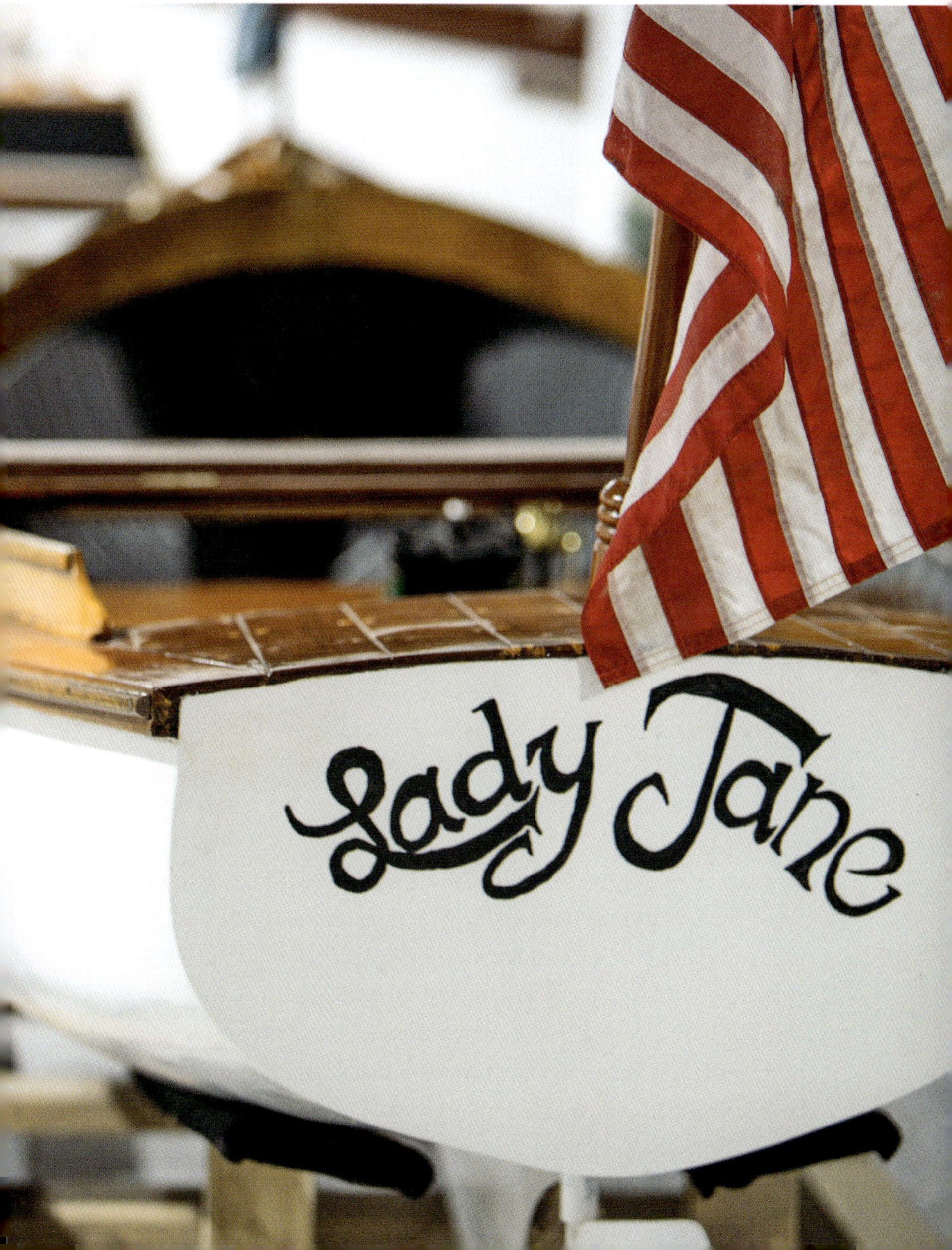

10 Bool's Flower Shop

Where all the flowers have gone

In the late 1800s, a wave of individualist anarchism started catching on in America. It was a pushback against the rise of big industry, government authority, and social inequality. To its followers, the movement stood for personal freedom and the rejection of imposed authority.

Born in England in 1846, Henry Bool arrived in Ithaca in 1872. During his 30 years in the city, he was a successful commercial developer – and the town's leading anarchist! Launching one enterprise after another, he developed land, built houses (furnished from his own furniture factory), and operated a flourishing dairy business. In 1894, he established Bool's Flower Shop, supported by the extensive greenhouses he built to grow flowers year-round.

During his whirlwind career, Bool began reading and adopting the philosophy of the American anarchists as his own, financially supporting other followers and their publications, and distributing pamphlets called "Liberty Luminants." He returned to England after the turn of the century, leaving behind a street near the Cornell campus that bears his name, and the flower shop that survives as one of the oldest continually operated businesses in the region.

Over several generations, the shop has passed through a small circle of local proprietors. And for 25 years, Doreen Culver-Foss has been part artist, part botanist, part therapist and dedicated steward of the shop's cultural and business legacy. While the shop has changed locations over its lifetime, it's now firmly rooted on North Aurora Street. Step inside today's Bool's and, yes, you'll feel history in the air, a sense that this place has always been here. It's a gentle jumble of color and texture, seasonal bouquets, potted plants, pottery, and other small gifts. Behind the scenes, a spacious design studio buzzes with activity. Tools of the trade – floral snippers, knives, ribbons – rest neatly on the counters. Overall, the shop balances historic character with a functional florist workspace, a quiet constant in a corner of town.

Address 209 North Aurora Street, Ithaca, NY 14850, +1 (607) 272-8410, www.boolsflowershop.com | Getting there Follow Route 79 into downtown Ithaca, bear right onto Seneca Way, then right onto North Aurora Street | Hours Mon–Sat 9am–5pm | Tip Any mention of flowers in Ithaca usually includes "Flower Power," the award-winning flagship IPA of the Ithaca Beer Company, a legend in craft beer circles, named among "The 25 Most Important American Craft Beers Ever Brewed" (122 Ithaca Beer Drive, Ithaca, NY 14850, www.ithacabeer.com).

11 The Bridge Street Bridge

George Bailey's leap of faith

Folks in this sleepy town take their legacy seriously. Named for the series of small falls and rapids on the Seneca River that drain both Cayuga and Seneca Lakes, Seneca Falls became the inspiration for Bedford Falls, the fictional setting in one of the most beloved films in cinema history.

It's a Wonderful Life is the heartwarming story of George Bailey, head of the town's building and loan association, who, after funds go missing, contemplates suicide by jumping off a bridge over the rushing water. Before he can take the leap, an angel named Clarence jumps instead. After George rescues him, Clarence shows George what Bedford Falls would have been like if he had never been born.

A year before he began shooting the film, director and co-screenwriter Frank Capra stopped for a haircut in Seneca Falls on his way to join family in nearby Auburn. His visit would be responsible for the striking similarities between real life Seneca Falls and the film's Bedford Falls. In the 1940s, both Seneca Falls and cinematic Bedford Falls were familiar and enduring examples of small-town America. Both were mill towns with Victorian architecture, and the two had large Italian populations. Both had streets with grassy medians in the middle, and both had building and loan associations. Like Seneca Falls, the film puts the location of Bedford Falls near the upstate cities of Buffalo, Rochester, and Elmira. But Capra's most notable inspiration was the town's 1915 Bridge Street Bridge, spanning 150 feet over the Cayuga-Seneca Canal, replicated for the most dramatic scenes in the film. And a true-to-life event on April 12, 1917 foreshadowed the story, when Antonio Varacalli drowned while rescuing a young woman who had attempted suicide by jumping off the bridge.

If you're a fan of *It's a Wonderful Life*, walk across the bridge. You can almost imagine yourself in the movie.

Address Bridge Street, Seneca Falls, NY 13148 | Getting there Take Routes 5 & 20 into the city, drive to Fall Street, turn south onto Walnut Street – the bridge is straight ahead (parking at Canal Street) | Hours Unrestricted | Tip The nearby It's a Wonderful Life Museum includes items from the personal collection of Karolyn Grimes, the actress who played Zuzu Bailey in the film (32 Fall Street, Seneca Falls, NY 13148, www.wonderfullifemuseum.com).

12 Calendar Clock Company

Cutting-edge technology, circa 1865

In April of 1865, while Confederate General Robert E. Lee was surrendering his troops to Union General Ulysses S. Grant to end the Civil War, a technological innovation was quietly taking shape in Ithaca. That same April, Henry Bishop Horton was granted a patent for a perpetual mechanism that automatically changed the date, compensating for the varying lengths of months, as well as the peculiarities of February, including leap years, all while interacting with a clock's timekeeping function. Later that year, the Ithaca Calendar Clock Company began manufacturing clocks that allowed users to easily read both the time and date at a glance, revolutionizing timekeeping and calendar management for the next 50 years.

At its height, the company was one of the largest employers in the city, selling clocks to banks, schools, corporate offices, and liquor companies who used them as premiums and giveaways to their best customers. There were over 40 different models, in heights ranging from 16 to 72 inches. Designers and craftsmen used locally harvested walnut to fashion wooden housings that turned clocks into fine pieces of furniture. Yet, by the early 20th century, development and widespread adoption of more accurate and reliable clocks and watches reduced the need for specialized calendar clocks, and by 1917, the company ceased operation, and its assets were sold off at public auction.

In 1981, the Ithaca Calendar Clock Company was revived by Michael Porter and two business partners, producing replicas of the original models, rejuvenating interest in the historic brand while preserving its legacy. Over the first 10 years, approximately 500 reproductions were made, true to the craftsmanship of the originals. Today, Porter repairs and refurbishes the old calendar clocks in an unmarked shop just south of Ithaca, where over 50 original calendar clocks are on display.

Address 1247 West Danby Road, Newfield, NY 14867, +1 (607) 339-7138, www.ithacacalendarclock.com | **Getting there** Follow Route 13 S out of Ithaca, then take Routes 96 and 34 (West Danby Road) to the unmarked shop (two buildings to the left of a convenience store) | **Hours** By appointment only | **Tip** Ithaca-based Tompkins Community Bank (originally the Tompkins County Trust Company, founded in 1836) displays a working Ithaca Calendar Clock in every one of its local branches (Main Office: 118 East Seneca Street, Ithaca, NY 14850, www.tompkinsbank.com).

13 A Carnegie Library

A little library with big dreams

He was the Bill Gates of his day. Andrew Carnegie was once the richest man in the world. Arriving in the US as a young immigrant from Scotland, he had built a vast steel empire by the 1880s – then gave it all away. He believed that wealthy individuals had a moral duty to give back to society, and he saw libraries as one of the most powerful resources for self-education. Beginning in 1886, he used his personal fortune to fund free public libraries throughout America.

The village of Penn Yan assembled a public library with 1,400 books, first in a local school, and later in the annex of the Presbyterian church. In 1902, Hatley K. Armstrong, the first president of the library, wrote to Carnegie's personal assistant, James Bertram, about the library's lack of its own building. A year later, Carnegie offered Penn Yan $10,000 for a library building, with the stipulation that a suitable site could be provided and $1,000 per year could be raised for stocking, maintenance, and operation of the library – standard requirements of "the Carnegie formula." A vote was taken, and school district residents voted 487 to 93 in favor of accepting Carnegie's gift.

The community raised $300 to purchase a lot on Main Street, originally the Hopkins Brothers furniture and coffin factory. New York architect Albert R. Ross was hired to design the building, and Jacob Allington & Sons, a local firm, became contractor for the dark-red-brick building with a portico entrance flanked by two Ionic columns.

Andrew Carnegie's philanthropic efforts led to the construction of 1,687 public libraries across the US, a total of 41 built in New York State outside of New York City. Of those libraries, the Penn Yan Library is the only existing one in the Finger Lakes. An expansion was completed in 1982, while the well-preserved original library structure now serves as the youth section, with picture books, early readers, chapter books, and an assortment of engaging non-fiction topics tailored for children.

Address 214 Main Street, Penn Yan, NY 14527, +1 (315) 536-6114, www.pypl.stls.org | Getting there From Route 54A (Elm Street), turn left onto Main Street | Hours Mon–Fri 9am–7:30pm, Sat 9am–4pm | Tip The Case Memorial-Seymour Library in Auburn was designed by Carrère and Hastings, who would later design the New York Public Library. The structure is an example of the Beaux Arts School of Architecture (176 Genesee Street, Auburn, NY 13021, www.seymourlibrary.org).

14 Castle Belhurst

Rooms with a boo!

In 1885, Carrie M. Harron, wife of a Manhattan banker, purchased property just south of Geneva, then known as "Bellehurst" (beautiful forest). After divorcing her husband, she married Captain Louis Dell Collins and began building a lavish mansion.

Designed by the renowned architectural firm Fuller & Wheeler, the extraordinary Romanesque Revival structure stands three stories tall and nine bays wide. It was constructed in distinctive Medina sandstone, with a one-story solarium, four stately rectangular stone chimneys, and an array of intricate details, including projecting porches, bay windows, towers crowned with conical and pyramidal roofs, and a *porte-cochère* with a bold Syrian arch. Fifty men worked for more than four years to erect the castle.

Carrie left the home to her grandson, who sold it to Cornelius J. "Red" Dwyer, bootlegger and gambling tycoon, who turned it into a club and gambling casino. During Prohibition, the club's liquor supply was run down from Canada using the canal system.

The historic castle is one of the most photographed buildings in the region, now home to its most famous haunted hotel, welcoming guests seeking the possibility of paranormal encounters. Belhurst's best known ghost is Isabella, an Italian diva, who, in a tangled love affair, fled with her forbidden lover to America. According to legend, her husband discovered that Mrs. Collins was secretly sheltering her at the castle. And once the lovers heard of his arrival, they attempted an escape through the underground wine cellar toward a waiting boat on the lake, but the tunnel collapsed, trapping Isabella inside.

On a visit here, stroll around the impeccable lakeside gardens, search for the bust of Captain Collins just outside the castle walls, and if you're here at dusk, you may catch sight of the bereft Isabella, dressed in white, roaming the grounds, grieving her lost lover.

Address 4069 West Lake Road, Geneva, NY 14456, +1 (315) 781-0201, www.belhurst.com | Getting there From Route 5 & 20 in Geneva, follow Route 14 south for 2 miles | Hours By permission | Tip Captain Collins also built the Collins Music Hall, constructed in a similar style to Belhurst, home to the 29th New York State Suffrage Convention of 1897. The building is now a student apartment house (459 South Main Street, Geneva, NY 14456).

15 Circus School

Become part of the show

Located beneath the iconic red banners and twinkling lights of Press Bay, where *The Ithaca Journal*, the community's daily newspaper, was once printed, Circus Culture is the region's only circus-performance school. The brainchild of Amy Cohen, who planted seeds for this enterprise during her student years at Ithaca College, the school officially opened in 2015. Equipped with two studio and performance rooms, high ceilings, aerial rings, and ample floor mats, the space supports a wide range of dynamic activities.

Attending Circus Culture isn't about running off to join the circus – it's about fostering life skills. Mastering the circus arts requires time, patience, and dedicated practice, instilling persistence and emphasizing the value of overcoming challenges – qualities that are valuable in many areas of life and work. Students of all ages and experience levels engage in workshops and classes, learning acrobatics, juggling, unicycling, and trapeze. These performance arts demand intense focus, a level of concentration that improves mental clarity and mindfulness.

The "Art of Clowning" class is led by experienced instructors, including Holly Adams, who has been teaching acting for 30 years and clowning for 20 years. These sessions emphasize physical comedy, improvisation, and character development. Participants engage in exercises that foster spontaneity, creativity, and authentic expression, all within a supportive and playful environment. Clowning creates a sense of childlike wonder and laughter, providing an escape from everyday stress.

Cohen explains that her students are encouraged to take risks in a society that often discourages mistakes, and Circus Culture collaborates with a variety of community organizations to expand opportunities for engagement. A series of summer performances further inspires students to push beyond their comfort zones.

Address 116 West Green Street, Ithaca, NY 14850, +1 (607) 269-7227, www.circusculture.org | Getting there Exiting the Commons onto North Cayuga Street, turn left, then turn right on East Green Street and right again into Press Bay Alley | Hours Some drop-in classes, but visit the website to see details of all classes and registration | Tip An entire room in the Ward O'Hara Agricultural Museum is dedicated to the work of Circus Model Builders, enthusiasts who build and display miniature circus models and dioramas. Featured is a miniature replica of the 1972 Hoxie Bros. Circus (6880 Route 38A, Auburn, NY 13021, www.wardwoharaagriculturalmuseum.org).

16 Confederate POW Camp

Prisoners called it "Hellmira"

During the American Civil War, thousands of captured soldiers endured squalid prison camps, with Camp Rathbun in Elmira emerging as one of the North's most notorious. Today, a quiet downtown neighborhood stands where rows of wooden barracks confined thousands of prisoners from 1864 to 1865. Nicknamed "Hellmira" by its inmates, the camp became infamous for its harsh and deadly conditions.

Hastily constructed, poorly planned, and originally designed to hold 6,000 prisoners, Barracks #3 was overwhelmed with 12,000. In that single year, 2,973 men perished due to insufficient food, rampant disease – including dysentery, typhoid, pneumonia, and smallpox – lack of medical care, and exposure during an unusually harsh winter.

To add insult to injury, an observation platform was built outside the prison camp across Water Street, and visitors were charged 10 cents to gawk at the prisoners. Refreshments were sold to spectators while the Confederate soldiers starved. Rather than ship the bodies of the Confederate dead home, Federal officials chose to bury the bodies adjacent to the city's Woodlawn Cemetery, and at the end of the war, surviving prisoners were required to take a loyalty oath before they were given a train ticket home.

The current site memorializes this tragic chapter in Elmira's past with a brass plaque set into a large flagstone at what was the main entrance to the camp. Behind a chain link fence you'll see a reconstructed barracks building that might have housed as many as 100 prisoners, and a section of the 12-foot stockyard wall with catwalk and sentry box, reimagining what once stood here during the last days of the Civil War. Building 1 lists the names of the prisoners, their rank, regiment, and cause of death. Three flagpoles tower over an interpretative display with a historical narrative, map, and map key to the former 30-acre compound.

Address 645 Winsor Avenue, Elmira, NY 14905, www.elmiracivilwar.org | Getting there Follow Church Street in downtown Elmira to Grove Street, then to Winsor Avenue | Hours Unrestricted (guided tours on Sat 10:30am–2:30pm) | Tip John W. Jones, an escaped slave, was responsible for the burial of the Confederate soldiers who died at the Elmira Prison Camp. A museum at his former home commemorates his life and work (1248 Davis Street, Elmira, NY 14901, www.johnwjonesmuseum.org).

17 Cortland Corset Mural

Celebrating a form-fitting legacy

A corset was a laced or hooked undergarment, reinforced with steel or whalebone. Tightening the corset constricted a woman's body to fit into the fashionable, thin-waisted dresses of the late 19th and early 20th centuries. For Victorian women, shaping the body into the desired hourglass figure conveyed modesty and discipline, reflecting values of self-restraint and moral virtue.

At one time, the city of Cortland was America's Corset Capital, and Cortland's handmade corsets were "unsurpassed for style, workmanship and durability." But before corsets, the 1869 double-brick building on East Court Street first housed the Cortland Wagon Company for the production of platform spring wagons and buggies. It was the largest and best-known maker of horse-drawn vehicles in America – until the arrival of the automobile.

During the 1920s, the Cortland Corset Company evolved into a burgeoning center for the production of ladies' undergarments, specializing in underbust corsets, corselets, and other foundational garments, providing employment for women, many of them Italian immigrants, skilled in pattern cutting and intricate hand stitching. However, as American women gained more independence, there was a shift toward more practical and comfortable clothing. The rigid and restrictive corset no longer suited women's active lifestyles.

Today, the Cortland Corset building has been repurposed as a small business incubator, including a gift shop and boutique, comic book shop, and yoga studio. One of the tenants is art educator Crystal Lyon of Living Illusion Studio, who designed and painted a dramatic three-story-tall mural on the west side of the building. Unveiled on September 29, 2018, "Grace," the steampunk-meets-Victoriana visual is a fusion of a 19th-century wagon wheel and a corset-attired woman, inspired by the legacies of the companies that once operated here.

Address 75 East Court Street, Cortland, NY 13045 | Getting there From Route 13, turn onto Greenbush Street, then onto East Court Street | Hours Unrestricted | Tip Cinch Art Space is a shop on the east side of the Cortland Corset building. Browse the range of locally made products, then visit the next room, where you'll see an original "Democrat" four-passenger wagon, manufactured here by the Cortland Wagon Company.

18 Custom Automotive

Sanctuary of automobilia

As you travel along Route 318 outside of Seneca Falls, don't hesitate to pull over when this place catches your eye. You won't know exactly what it is at first. The sign reads "Custom Auto," but the urge to discover more is irresistible. You gaze at a motley collection of cars in varying states of preservation, some from as early as the 1920s, some running and some not, some in rusted heaps, others only in parts, scattered around the five-acre property.

Slumbering among the relics are some vintage models, from a 1934 Ford pickup truck to a 1938 Chevrolet Master Deluxe sedan. They're just a few of over a hundred or so vehicles, including taxis, tow trucks, limousines, tractors, motorcycles, golf carts, and a Wayne County Sheriff's patrol car, its paint peeling, but still holding onto its history. A replica of the General Lee Dodge Charger from *The Dukes of Hazzard* television show is displayed prominently out front. The scene is one of faded glory, where each vehicle tells a story.

A dozen retro gas pumps stand like sentinels, guarding memories of another era, flanked by countless vintage signs, fire hydrants, and oil cans. And for some reason, there are a couple of goats in a pen and a few chickens and ducks roaming around the yard.

Walk inside the repair shop – you've entered a time capsule, where you might hear an old car engine rumble back to life. The room is overflowing with an eclectic jumble of automotive tools and parts fighting for space with moose heads, sleds, parking meters, and traffic signals. You can hardly believe your eyes.

This sanctuary of automobilia and curiosities is the 20-years-in-the-making creation of Alfred Ritz (no relation to the hotels or the crackers), a second-generation mechanic who enjoys bringing old cars back from the brink, and who claims he didn't set out to create a roadside attraction. It just happened.

Address 2166 Route 318, Seneca Falls, NY 13148, +1 (315) 730-9506, www.facebook.com/customautosenecafalls | **Getting there** From Seneca Falls, take Route 20 to Route 318 | **Hours** Mon–Fri 9am–5pm | **Tip** In 1976, a life-sized sculpture of a classic Volkswagen bug was assembled nearly entirely of stones, the obsession of Cornell art professor Stephen Gibbian. Search for the nearly hidden *Stone Volkswagen* at the intersection of Ringwood and Mineah/Midline Roads, just outside of Ithaca.

19 Dio Way

Flash the devil horns

Naming a street after one of a town's native sons is a meaningful way for a community to honor and memorialize an individual who's made significant contributions, either locally or on a larger scale. Ronnie James Dio accomplished both, and on November 15, 1998, the city of Cortland officially renamed a street "Dio Way" in his honor.

Born in 1942 in Portsmouth, New Hampshire, Ronald James Padavona spent many of his formative years in Cortland. Beginning with his first band, the Vegas Kings, formed while attending Cortland High School, his musical career spanned six decades with Ronnie and the Rumblers, Ronnie and the Red Caps, Ronnie Dio and the Prophets, Elf, The Electric Elves, The Elves, Rainbow, Black Sabbath, Dio, and Heaven and Hell. Even after his death in 2010, his influence continues to be felt through the many musicians he inspired, including Metallica, Iron Maiden, and Judas Priest. With his powerful voice and theatrical storytelling, Dio helped elevate heavy metal into an art form.

Oh, and about the "devil horns" gesture: perhaps Dio's most lasting contribution to rock and metal culture. It involves extending the index and pinky fingers while tucking in the middle and ring fingers. Dio adopted the hand sign from his Italian grandmother, who used it to ward off the "evil eye" in Italian folk tradition. He began using the gesture during his time with Black Sabbath (after replacing Ozzy Osbourne), and it became a connection to the darker or more aggressive themes in heavy metal music.

Dio Way, although not far from his boyhood home, feels like an ironic tribute. It's a short, austere block, in stark contrast to the artist's energy and creativity. Under the street sign you might see flowers, candles, or even guitar picks, left there in honor of Dio's legacy. It's a landmark that draws devoted fans who flash the devil horns when they drive by.

Address Dio Way, between Central Avenue and East Court Street, Cortland, NY 13045, www.cortland.org | Getting there From Route 13, turn onto Hubbard Street, follow to Central Avenue, then turn onto Dio Way | Hours Unrestricted | Tip Another musician with roots in the region, Peter Yarrow rented an apartment on East State Street in Ithaca while attending Cornell, where he composed "Puff, the Magic Dragon," popularized by Peter, Paul and Mary in 1963 (614 East State Street, Ithaca, NY 14850).

20 Dr. Foster's Cottage

Where sulphur turned to gold

The early practice of hydrotherapy arrived here in 1849, when Dr. Henry Foster acquired 10 acres of land that encompassed the legendary sulfur-rich springs earlier used by Native American healers, who believed the water had miraculous and spiritual powers.

Opened on September 13, 1850, with a waiting list, Clifton Springs Water Cure began as a modest cluster of wooden structures. As its popularity grew, the demand for expanded facilities followed. Construction of a second set of buildings, made of brick, was started in 1856 and, when completed in 1871, became known as the Clifton Springs Sanitarium. Over the years, thousands of people came to enjoy the sulphur waters and natural therapies for a wide variety of conditions, both as "medicine" as well as rejuvenation and relaxation.

Originally built in 1854, the gingerbread cottage that once served as Dr. Foster's home now houses the Clifton Springs Historical Society Museum. Fascinating exhibits, including early medical instruments, photos of the site's historic buildings, items related to the local nursing school, a mannequin dressed in a nursing outfit designed by Mrs. Foster, and even one of Dr. Foster's desks provide a window into the remarkable story of the town and the legacy of the water cure.

On the wall above the cottage fireplace there's an original sketch that Robert Reid produced for the Red Cross. The Sanitarium's most famous patient, Reid, an Impressionist painter and muralist, came to Clifton Springs in the 1920s for treatment after suffering a severe paralytic stroke that paralyzed the right side of his body. It was here where the artist, determined to continue his art, began to resume his work by learning to paint with his left hand.

Interest in bathing in the sulphur springs has experienced a resurgence, prompting the local hospital to dedicate an entire wing to therapeutic water treatments.

Address 9 East Main Street, Clifton Springs, NY 14432, +1 (315) 462-7394, www.fostercottage.org | Getting there From the New York Thruway (I-90), take Interchange 42 into Clifton Springs | Hours Tue–Fri 10am–4pm (Sep–May), Wed–Sat 10am–4pm (Jun–Aug) | Tip Across the sulphur brook that flows through Clifton Springs, a historical marker honoring Dr. Foster stands outside the imposing five-story brick edifice built in 1896 to house 190 patients in the former Clifton Springs Sanitarium (11 East Main Street, Clifton Springs, NY 14432).

21 Dutch Schultz Hideout

Prohibition era's notorious gangster

New York State Senator and president of the Groton Mechanics' Bank, Benn Conger was on a train to Albany in 1909 when he encountered a fellow passenger with a portable typewriter. Captivated by the ingenuity and potential of the groundbreaking device, Conger bought the patents and manufacturing rights from the inventor and moved the Standard Typewriter Company from New York City to Groton. One of the new company's first customers was Theodore Roosevelt, who took Model #2 with him on a big game hunting trip to Africa.

With the success of a company now called the Corona Typewriting Company, and with his financial windfall, Conger purchased an 18-acre property in the village, and in 1921, completed building a 10-bedroom Colonial Revival mansion. Sadly, he lived in the home only a few months before his death in early 1922.

Conger's mansion was later rented to one of the Prohibition era's most notorious gangsters, Arthur Flegenheimer, better known as Dutch Schultz, a bootlegger who controlled a significant portion of illicit liquor distribution in New York City. Seeking a safe haven outside the city, the "Beer Baron" moved his base of operations to rural Groton where he could manage his criminal enterprises while evading law enforcement efforts to apprehend him. Schultz made millions from his operations, but on the night of October 23, 1935, he was gunned down in Newark's Palace Chop House tavern along with three of his associates.

Over the following years, the estate has weathered several changes in ownership, first as a private residence, then beginning in 1978, as a bed and breakfast. Following multiple innkeepers over the years, the Benn Conger Inn is currently in the hands of the Brennan family, who welcome guests for overnight accommodations, as well as sightseers captivated by the inn's rich history and its intriguing connection to the infamous Dutch Schultz.

Address 206 West Cortland Street, Groton, NY 13073, +1 (607) 898-5817, www.thebenncongerinn.com | Getting there From Route 13 between Ithaca and Cortland, take Route 38 past Freeville and into Groton, then left onto Cortland Street | Hours By appointment only | Tip The former residence of Joseph "Joe the Barber" Barbara in the sleepy hamlet of Apalachin (one hour away) was the site of a historic organized crime summit in 1957. The estate is now Hidden Farm, a horse boarding and lesson facility (625 McFall Street, Apalachin, NY 13732).

22 Educated Golf Course

Take a swing at this historic course

British-born Robert Trent Jones moved with his family to Rochester, New York at the age of five. As a young man, he worked as a caddie at the Country Club of Rochester and later at the Sodus Bay Heights Golf Club. After taking up the game, he achieved the top amateur score at the 1927 Canadian Open and set a course record at the club.

Jones was accepted at Cornell University in 1928, where an unconventional course of study allowed him to pursue his interest in golf course design. It would be the country's first program dedicated to golf architecture. While taking classes in landscape architecture, agronomy, horticulture, hydraulics, surveying, public speaking, and economics, he found time to design the back nine holes of the university golf course. Opened in 1941, it was meant to inspire interest in the sport among the student body. Thirteen years later, he returned to complete the first nine holes.

Jones claimed the course would require the use of every club in the bag, and his design was intended to be a difficult par but an easy bogey. He took particular delight in the sixth hole, a par three. Both visually striking and technically demanding, the fairway descends to a green bordered by water along the right side and encircled by bunkers. The elevation drop from tee to green adds complexity to club selection, while the water hazard calls for a bit of daring. It's a classic Jones design, blending natural beauty with sophisticated golf course architecture. The course is home to the Big Red varsity team and open to the public. The facility includes practice greens, chipping area, practice sand trap, and a 300-yard driving range.

Jones went on to become the world's most prolific golf designer, creating 350 courses and renovating another 150. His papers, mementos, personal documents, and course designs are housed at the Rare and Manuscript Collections at Cornell.

Address 213 Warren Road, Ithaca, NY 14850, +1 (607) 254-6531, www.golfatcornell.com | Getting there From downtown Ithaca, follow Route 13 north, turn right onto Warren Road | Hours Visit website to book a tee time | Tip Mark Twain once said, "Golf is a good walk spoiled," so he would probably be surprised that an 18-hole miniature golf course at Eldridge Park bears his name (96 Eldridge Park Drive, Elmira, www.eldridgepark.org).

23 Eight Square Schoolhouse

If only the eight walls could talk

Octagonal houses were popularized in the United States during the mid-19th century by phrenologist Orson Squire Fowler of Cohocton in Steuben County, who touted the advantages over rectangular and square structures in his widely publicized book, *The Octagon House: A Home For All, or A New, Cheap, Convenient, and Superior Mode of Building*. Today, by most estimates, fewer than 500 octagon buildings remain standing, a good many of them still dotting the Finger Lakes countryside.

In 1827, Tompkins County trustees voted to replace the wooden plank school of District #5 with a new school built with bricks. They hired Henry Balcom from nearby McLean to build a school that would be "twenty eight feet in the clear and eight square," an idea influenced by local settlers, originally from the Delaware Valley, who were familiar with the Quaker schools. Well before the octagon craze, Quaker communities in southeastern Pennsylvania had embraced the simplicity of the octagonal form for school buildings.

The forward-thinking design had windows to supply light from every direction, and heat came from a wood-burning cast-iron stove in the center of the room. Brick walls helped to retain heat during the cold months and provide insulation against the heat in the warm weather.

Local folks call it the "Ink Bottle," since it resembles the eight-sided ink bottles once used by schoolkids to dip their writing quills in. The Eight Square School served children of the district until 1941 when the Dryden School District centralized and began busing the children into Dryden or Freeville to attend school. The building was used as a community center and meeting place for another 10 years, and in 1955, ownership of the school was transferred to what is now The History Center of Tompkins County. The center hosts group, classroom, and homeschool visits during both the fall and spring terms.

Address 1756 Hanshaw Road, Ithaca, NY 14850, +1 (607) 273-8284 | Getting there Follow Route 13 N from Ithaca, then right onto Hanshaw Road | Hours By appointment only; to request a tour, email eightsquare@thehistorycenter.net | Tip Among several octagonal structures in the Finger Lakes, the Circus House in Homer may be the most unusual. Built in 1902 as the winter home for the Sig Sautelle Circus, the building was designed to train circus animals on the main floor while housing them in the basement during the winter off-season (161 South Main Street, Route 11, Homer, NY 13077).

24 Electric Chair at Swaby's

A shocking discovery

Amelia Gould Swaby, daughter of Seabury S. Gould, founder of Goulds Pumps, widow of Dr. William Swaby, one of the region's leading surgeons, and neighbor of suffragette Elizabeth Cady Stanton, purchased the site of a blacksmith shop in 1912 after a fire destroyed the original structure, and built this three-story, Federal-style, red-brick building. Over its storied past, this has been home to a variety of enterprises, including the International School of Beauty, Weddigen's Restaurant, Andrews Grocery, and as of 1999, a local watering hole that goes by the name of Swaby's Tavern. The whimsical gargoyles perched on the building's façade hint at what awaits within.

The brainchild of local entrepreneur and antique dealer Michael Dwyer, Swaby's has changed hands a few times, and is now entrusted to Anthony and Michael Pacini, saloonkeepers and curators of a place that feels more like an enchanting museum or an oddity-filled attic than a neighborhood tavern.

The eclectic mix of memorabilia and rescued treasures includes movie posters and props, quirky taxidermy and trophy heads, a barber chair, street signs, chandeliers, stained-glass windows, a mummy sarcophagus, life preservers from the *Titanic*, a Picasso lithograph – and one very bizarre piece. It's an electric chair, rumored to be a back-up to "Old Sparky," the infamous chair built in the Auburn Prison cabinet shop for the first-ever execution by electrocution in 1890. Swaby's chair is secured in a chamber behind original cell bars discarded after a 1929 riot in the prison. Surrounding walls are plastered with electrocution documents, newspaper clippings, mug shots, fingerprint cards, and license plates made by prison inmates.

On a visit to this extraordinary place, allow the history of Auburn to seep in, then fortify yourself with a hearty meal accompanied by a tasty libation or two.

Address 6 South Street, Auburn, NY 13021, +1 (315) 252-5400, www.swabystavern.com | **Getting there** Follow South Street (Route 38) to the Genesee Street intersection; the tavern is next door to the Phoenix Building | **Hours** Mon–Fri 11am–11pm, Sat & Sun noon–11pm | **Tip** Beginning at Swaby's, a sidewalk tour takes you along South Street, past the homes of Auburn's most notable citizens, including the Seward House, Case Mansion, Queen's and King's Court, John Foster Dulles Mansion, and the Harriet Tubman Home.

25 Elmira Drive-In Theater

But is anyone watching the movie?

John Wayne, as Quirt Evans, is a gunfighter on the run, injured when his horse stumbles near a Quaker family's land. The family takes him in, and as he regains his health, he falls for the daughter, Penelope, played by Gail Russell. Will he give up his outlaw life for a future with Penelope? *Angel and the Badman* was the feature attraction at the opening of the Elmira Drive-In on April 16, 1949.

Local folks buzzed with excitement. Families flocked here to enjoy double features, popcorn, and the novelty of watching movies from the comfort of their cars. It was convenient and affordable, a weekend destination not just for parents and children, but also for teenage couples seeking some privacy. Residing on 19 acres of land, almost halfway between the city of Elmira and the town of Big Flats, the drive-in has had a complicated history. Opened with a single screen and 13 ramps for 500 cars with in-car speakers, it was first simply named "Drive-In Theatre." As the decades rolled on, its popularity began to wane. The opening of a multiplex cinema at the nearby Arnot Mall in 1967, along with the rise of home video, reduced attendance. The Elmira drive-in, like many others around the country, struggled to compete. Ownership changed hands multiple times as each new proprietor tried to find a winning formula to keep the business afloat.

Zurich Cinemas became the owners in 2008, intent on restoring the drive-in to its former glory. Modern digital projection equipment was installed, FM transmitters were upgraded to Dolby Stereo surround sound, and offerings from the snack bar expanded.

The Covid-19 pandemic in 2020 brought an unexpected twist to the drive-in's story. While traditional cinemas faced significant challenges, the drive-in was a safe, socially distanced entertainment option. The Elmira Drive-In saw record attendance numbers, breathing life back into the old gal.

Address 2431 Route 352, Elmira, NY 14903, +1 (607) 734-8599, www.elmiradrivein.com | Getting there Follow Route 86 W from Elmira; in Big Flats, exit onto Route 352 and drive for 2 miles | Hours After dark, Apr–Oct – visit website for showtimes | Tip The Hal Roach Pavilion in Elmira's Grove Park is named for the city's native son, who became a Hollywood producer, best known for partnering Stan Laurel and Oliver Hardy, and the *Our Gang* comedy series (714 Grove Street, Elmira, NY 14903, www.chemunghistory.com/hal-roach).

26 Emmeline's Fountain

Icon on Main Street

In 1846, William Wolcott Wadsworth, of the prominent Genesee Valley Wadsworths, married Emmeline Austin of Boston. They became the parents of three sons, William, Livingston, and Herbert, and after her husband died suddenly in 1852, Emmeline was left to raise the boys on her own. When their mother passed away, the Wadsworth boys honored her memory with a gift to the village. Emmeline was a passionate animal lover, so the brothers decided that a stately horse-watering fountain would be a fitting tribute.

They commissioned renowned architect Richard Morris Hunt, designer of the base of the Statue of Liberty and the façade of the Metropolitan Museum of Art in New York, to design the circular granite fountain, and French sculptor Antoine-Louis Barye, distinguished for his work as an *animalier* (animal sculptor), to craft a bronze bear at the top. The fountain was installed in the center of town to great fanfare and ceremony in 1888.

Originally a place where travelers stopped to refresh their horses, the Emmeline Wadsworth Fountain has since evolved into a cherished symbol of the village, affectionately called "Emmeline." According to local legend, the fountain was built and generously deeded to the town by the sons with one condition – if the bear was ever removed or harmed, it would revert back to the Wadsworth heirs.

Over the years, the fountain has been the subject of countless photographs, occasional auto mishaps, a rite of passage for local college students' late-night swimming sessions, and acts of vandalism. In the late 1960s, someone made off with Emmeline in the dead of night. The following morning, with the fountain now missing the bear, the State Police were called in, and a full investigation began. Two students from SUNY Geneseo were identified as the culprits, their families were forced to pay damages, and Emmeline was reinstated to her rightful place on Main Street.

Address Main Street, Geneseo, NY 14454, www.geneseony.org | Getting there From either Mount Morris Road or South Street, turn onto Main Street | Hours Unrestricted | Tip The Wadsworth Homestead, the only country manor estate in New York State continually owned by the original family since 1804, holds priceless treasures from seven generations of Wadsworths (4 South Street, Geneseo, NY 14454, www.wadsworthhomestead.com).

27 Empire Haven Nudist Park

Naked and unafraid

The Germans call it *freikörperkultur*, which translates as "free body culture." It's a lifestyle that includes communal, open-air nudity as part of enjoying nature. In America, the naturism movement and naturist gatherings began in the 1930s and grew steadily during the 1940s and '50s.

In 1959, George and Mary Robinson purchased 100 acres of rural land, a mix of cow pastures, apple orchards and strawberry fields, and opened Empire Haven, the first nudist park in New York. Located just outside the hamlet of Moravia, the secluded park is now operated by the third generation of the Robinson family. It remains one of the few naturist enclaves in all of the state.

The setting is a gated community, deep in the countryside, with overnight accommodations that range from rental trailers and cabins to a variety of RV sites, many with electric and water hook-ups. For a more nature-immersed experience, adventurers can opt to pitch their own tents in designated areas. Visitors leave their pretenses at the door, along with their clothes. From late spring to early fall, they sunbathe in the open air to acquire borderless tans, swim without bathing suits, play tennis and volleyball without the benefit of uniforms. They relax in the hot tub or sauna, pitch horseshoes, play shuffleboard, or pickleball, and hike along a nature trail. And there's a snack bar for food in the nude. Nudity is optional everywhere except in the pool area, sauna, and hot tub.

The tranquil and scenic surroundings foster a welcoming, inclusive atmosphere for individuals and families of all backgrounds and ages, encouraging a connection to nature, a sense of community, and a shared, liberating experience. Empire Haven adheres to the philosophy of *freikörperkultur*, with an emphasis on body positivity and personal comfort. Unwind and undress. Shed your garments, and don't forget the sunscreen.

Address 5947 Sun Lane, Moravia, NY 13118, +1 (315) 497-0135, www.empirehaven.net | **Getting there** From the village of Moravia, follow Skinner Hill Road to Lick Street, then turn right onto Sun Lane | **Hours** Daily May 15–Sept 15 Shoulder Season Sun–Sat 9am–3pm, Memorial Day–Labor Day Sun–Thu 9am–3pm, Fri & Sat 9am–5pm | **Tip** Potter's Falls, a 25-foot waterfall in Six Mile Gorge, is an unofficial naturist sanctuary in Ithaca. The deep pool below the falls is a popular skinny-dipping hole, and there are rock ledges for nude sunbathing (Giles Street, Ithaca, NY 14850).

28 Enfield CCC Camp

Roosevelt's New Deal legacy

During the Great Depression, with nearly one-third of the country's workforce unemployed, President Franklin Roosevelt created a public work-relief program called the Civilian Conservation Corps. Under the guidance of the Departments of the Interior and Agriculture, a CCC camp was established near the Old Mill in Enfield.

The site was the 387-acre parcel donated by Robert H. Treman in 1920 for the development of a public park, and from 1933 to 1941, more than 100 young men worked here, improving trails, building stone bridges and stairways, and planting trees, shrubs and grass throughout the park. You can still find initials and names of some of these men inscribed in the cliff walls along the trails, and if you hike the trail behind the gristmill, you'll pass the spot where they lived in wooden barracks. Across the creek, you can see a stone chimney, all that's left of the superintendent's cabin.

The Old Mill, a water-powered gristmill, served the community from 1839 to 1916, grinding wheat grown by nearby farmers, and early in the 1920s, was restored and converted to a pavilion. Today the mill houses exhibits describing the workings of the mill, the role it played in the surrounding agricultural settlement, as well as the story and photos of the young men of the Civilian Conservation Corps.

The park itself stands as one of the region's essential destinations with rugged Enfield Glen gorge, carved as glaciers receded from Central New York, as its crown jewel. Winding trails, constructed by the gangs of the CCC, trace the gorge's path, leading visitors past a dozen stunning waterfalls, including Lucifer Falls, cascading down 115 feet of rock face. Take the upper trail for a spectacular view of Lucifer Falls from above. Generations of photographers, artists, writers, and poets have found inspiration and contemplation in this remarkable place.

Address 129 Upper Park Road, Newfield, NY 14867, +1 (607) 273-3440, www.parks.ny.gov/parks/roberttreman | Getting there From Route 13, take Enfield Falls Road (Route 327) to the upper park | Hours Unrestricted | Tip Before the Treman era, Edward K. Tryon, a 19th century tycoon whose Philadelphia company was the largest sporting goods retailer in the United States and probably the world, made Enfield Glen his summer home. He not only built a home here, he owned the local hotel and entire glen property, including Lucifer Falls.

29 Ezra Cornell's Sarcophagus

The founder's final resting place

Ezra Cornell was hired by Samuel Morse, the inventor of the telegraph, initially to help lay the first telegraph lines. When that proved impractical, Cornell proposed stringing the wires on glass-insulated poles above ground. He went on to build a network across the northeastern United States. Choosing to accept much of his payment in stock, Ezra eventually became the largest shareholder in Western Union. The telegraph's success made him a very wealthy man, allowing him to establish Cornell University in 1865.

Cornell passed away in 1874, just nine years after founding his university, and was buried at Lake View Cemetery, overlooking Cayuga Lake. That same year saw the completion of Sage Chapel, designed in Victorian Gothic style by Charles Babcock, Cornell's first professor of architecture, a gift of Henry W. Sage, an Ithacan who had made his fortune in the lumber business.

In 1883, a mortuary antechapel was added to serve as the final resting place for important members of the Cornell community, and William Wetmore Story, an American neoclassicist sculptor, who worked in Rome, received a commission to make a recumbent portrait sculpture of Ezra. Upon completion of the work and its arrival in Ithaca, Cornell's remains were moved from the cemetery to Sage Chapel and interred within an ornate sarcophagus, adorned with Story's remarkable sculpture, unveiled at the university in the fall of 1885.

Today, the crypt holds the bodies or ashes of 14 individuals: founders Ezra Cornell and Andrew Dickson White and their wives, New York Governor Alonzo B. Cornell and his wife, two infant children of White, trustee John McGraw, benefactress Jennie McGraw Fiske, university librarian Willard Fiske, President Edmund Ezra Day and his wife, and President Deane Malott. The apse at the east end of the chapel separately holds the remains of Henry Sage and his wife.

Address Ho Plaza, Cornell University, Ithaca, NY 14853, +1 (607) 255-4214, www.cornell.edu | **Getting there** From Stewart Avenue in Ithaca, drive to the Campus Road parking and information booth; Ho Plaza is a pedestrian walkway | **Hours** Daily 9am–6pm | **Tip** Ezra Cornell recruited skilled craftsmen from all over Europe to build a Victorian Gothic stone villa called Llenroc (Cornell spelled backwards); however, he died before the building was completed. Since 1911, it has been the home of Delta Phi fraternity (100 Cornell Avenue, Ithaca, NY 14850).

30 Fillmore's Log Cabin

A past president's humble beginnings

Millard Fillmore was born on January 7, 1800, in a log cabin near what is now the town of Moravia, spending much of his youth clearing land and raising crops on the family's tenant farm. At age 18, he began to read law, and after being admitted to the bar, practiced law in Buffalo. He served as a member of the House of Representatives, and in 1848, was elected Vice President on a ticket with Zachary Taylor. When Taylor died suddenly only 16 months into his term, Fillmore became the 13th President of the United States.

Very few locations in the country can lay claim to an American president, and Moravia is proud to be among them – the town's picturesque park is named after him. Visit Fillmore Glen State Park for the picnic and camping grounds, natural swimming area, and wooded hiking trails, but don't miss a replica of his birth home, a log cabin just off the parking area. The cabin's two first-floor rooms are visible to visitors through glass panels, furnished as they would have been in the original cabin, including a kitchen area next to the fireplace set with dining utensils, a small cradle, a table with books, a pair of reading glasses, and a ladder to the second-floor sleeping quarters.

As unlucky president number 13, Fillmore would go on to lose his bid for the Whig Party nomination for a full term in 1852, and fail four years later as the Know-Nothing Party's candidate. He's often been cast as an inconsequential president and nearly forgotten, except for an article by H. L. Mencken in *The New York Evening Mail* on December 28, 1917. Mencken's satirical piece credited Fillmore as the first president to install a bathtub in the White House, a tongue-in-cheek essay that nonetheless was circulated as fact.

In honor of the "bathtub hoax," the town of Moravia celebrates annual Fillmore Days every summer with four-wheeled bathtub races down Main Street.

Address 1686 Route 38, Moravia, NY 13118, +1 (315) 497-0130, www.parks.ny.gov/parks/fillmoreglen | Getting there Follow South Main Street (Route 38) out of downtown Moravia | Hours Daily mid Apr – mid Nov during daylight hours | Tip John D. Rockefeller, founder of the Standard Oil Company and one of the world's wealthiest men, grew up in Moravia. A historical marker at the intersection of Rockefeller Road and Firelane 33, is the site of his boyhood home.

31 Firebrand Books Building

LGBTQ+ community landmark

Ithaca has a rich and enduring history of LGBTQ+ rights advocacy and activism. In 1968, a student-led boycott at Morrie's Bar in Collegetown protested the bar owner's policy of harassing gay patrons and discouraging their trade. It was the first gay student sit-in in the United States. The Student Homophile League formed at Cornell University in 1968 was only the second public gay student organization in the country. Local gay activists participated in New York City's first Gay Pride March in June 1970 on the first anniversary of the Stonewall Riots, wearing T-shirts they had silk-screened outside the campus chapel. And 10 years later, Ithaca became one of the first cities in the country to prohibit discrimination by landlords, employers, and businesses based on sexual orientation.

Firebrand Books was established in Ithaca in 1984 by pioneer publisher Nancy Bereano, a lesbian and feminist activist, producing fiction and non-fiction works by women of color, women coming out of poverty, trans women, the genderqueer, and other marginalized voices. It was located on the second floor of an 1872 building on the Ithaca Commons pedestrian mall, better known to Ithacans as the Home Dairy building, with a former bakery on the ground floor.

Firebrand published some of the most influential works of queer literature after World War II, including Alison Bechdel's *Dykes to Watch Out For*, but changing economics of the book trade forced it to close in 2000.

In 2022, the Ithaca Landmarks Preservation Commission recommended designation of the building as a local landmark; however, the building's current owner, a religious group openly opposed to homosexuality, refused to allow the placement of a plaque on the building itself, leading to a campaign to establish a marker on the Commons. In 2024, the historical marker was installed in view of the former Firebrand Books building.

Address 143 East State Street, Ithaca, NY 14860, www.cityofithaca.org | **Getting there** Follow Route 79 (East State Street) into downtown Ithaca | **Hours** Unrestricted, viewable from the outside only | **Tip** Across from the Firebrand building, a life-sized bronze casting depicts Ithaca native Erin Schlather seated at a café table, with a cup of coffee and two books. The table's edge bears the words "Child of Ithaca, Citizen of the World." An empty chair invites passersby to join her for a cup of coffee.

32 First Wave Sculptures

Birthplace of American feminism

In 1848, a group of "uppity women" from Seneca Falls banded together to make "unladylike" demands, for things like property rights, child custody rights, equal access to education, equal pay for equal work, the right to own property, the right to control their earnings, and – gasp! – the right to vote.

It took the form of a convention, organized by Elizabeth Cady Stanton, Lucretia Mott, Mary Ann M'Clintock, Jane Hunt, Martha Coffin Wright, and Amelia Bloomer, motivated by their own life experiences. Over two days, July 19 and 20, more than 300 people attended the first Women's Rights Convention in the local Wesleyan Chapel.

Initially drafted by Cady Stanton, a document called the Declaration of Sentiments and Resolutions, echoing the language and cadence of the Declaration of Independence, called for equal social, legal, and political rights for women. Signed by 68 women and 32 men, including abolitionist Frederick Douglass, the Declaration became a blueprint for the early women's rights movement.

The national park is actually a collection of historic sites, all within easy walking distance. The centerpiece of the visitors center is a 20-figure sculpture executed by Lloyd Lillie, Professor of Fine Arts at Boston University, near-life-sized depictions of the assembled activists, installed and dedicated in 1993. Called *The First Wave*, referring to the earliest period of organized activism, the installation allows you to feel as if you were part of that 1848 gathering, as you mingle among the bronze figures. Take a walk up the metal stairs to browse multiple exhibits that tell the "herstory" of the movement, the legend of the local activists, the battle for the ballot, and the life and times of women of the era.

The park includes the Wesleyan Chapel, the farmhouse Elizabeth Cady Stanton called "Grassmere," and Mary Ann M'Clintock's two-story red-brick home.

Address Women's Rights National Historical Park, 136 Fall Street (Routes 5 & 20), Seneca Falls, NY 13148, +1 (315) 568-0024, www.nps.gov | Getting there Follow Routes 5 & 20 into downtown Seneca Falls, between Clinton Street and Mynderse Street | Hours Daily 10am–4pm | Tip Visit the nearby National Women's Hall of Fame on the first floor of the historic Seneca Knitting Mill, featuring ongoing exhibitions on loan from the Smithsonian art installation (1 Canal Street, Seneca Falls, NY 13148, www.womenofthehall.org).

33 Forest Bathing

Thoreau would approve

Henry David Thoreau once wisely wrote, "An early morning walk is a blessing for the whole day." Thoreau would undoubtedly embrace the practice of forest bathing, or *shinrin-yoku,* a term coined in Japan in the 1980s as a preventive healthcare method. This is not exercise, hiking, or jogging. It's more about being in the present moment and connecting with nature.

The forested trails of the Finger Lakes are defining elements of the region's character, with diverse ecosystems, breathtaking views, and access to remote, peaceful settings. Since 2016, the Bristol Hills Trail near Naples has provided a natural environment for guided immersions that transform simple walks into curated, meaningful, and restorative experiences. The guide is Deborah Denome, horticultural therapist, herbalist, and certified forest therapy guide, trained in techniques and practices that help participants fully engage with sensory elements of the forest in ways that provide an inner calm and fresh inspiration. Leave your phone and cameras behind.

Deborah serves as a bridge between participants and nature, creating personalized excursions, based on individual comfort levels, experiences that might be harder to achieve independently. She offers prompts or cues called "invitations," encouraging participants to focus attention, perhaps listening for certain sounds or observing specific natural details of the wooded landscape. One invitation might be to notice the different melodies and rhythms a stream makes as it meanders alongside the trail. Another might suggest slowing way down and noticing all the living things that are moving even more slowly than you are. These invitations create a serene escape, in stark contrast to often stressful patterns of daily life.

Finger Lakes Forest Therapy sessions are 90-minute or 3-hour guided walks, concluding with a tea ceremony.

Address 6141 Hicks Road, Naples, NY 14512, +1 (585) 412-5550, www.flforesttherapy.com | Getting there Follow Route 21 south along the west side of Canandaigua Lake to Hicks Road | Hours Visit website for details of walks and retreats | Tip After learning forest bathing practices, visit the Fischer Old Growth Forest Trail, along a pre-European settlement area. It's a mix of old agricultural fields and forests with trees over 150 feet tall and 300 years old (1349 Route 13, Newfield, NY 14867).

34 Fort Hill Cemetery

Grave encounters of the famous and infamous

The story of a cemetery that was once the home of Indigenous peoples is a narrative deeply entwined with history, culture, and the passage of time – this hallowed ground, now the Fort Hill Cemetery, was once a fortified village of the Cayugas. European settlers dedicated the hill overlooking the city of Auburn as a cemetery on July 7, 1852, and over the years it has provided resting places for historical figures, local heroes, war veterans, and the occasional inmate from Auburn Prison.

To honor the land's original inhabitants, a striking 56-foot-tall obelisk of native stone was erected to honor Chief Logan, Cayuga Nation orator and leader, who legend says was born at this site, but is not actually buried here. Inscribed on the monument are words he famously asked after his family was murdered by colonizers, "Who is there to mourn for Logan?"

A walking tour is a journey through history. You'll pass the marker for Harriet Tubman, the formerly enslaved abolitionist. You'll see the gravesites of Abraham Lincoln's Secretary of State William Henry Seward, buried there with his wife, daughter and granddaughter. You can pay your respects to Myles Keogh, who fought and died alongside General Custer at the Battle of Little Bighorn; John Hardenburg, Revolutionary War veteran, regarded as the founder of Auburn, having built the first mill on the Owasco outlet; Theodore Case, inventor of the first commercially successful soundtrack for motion pictures; Dr. Sylvester Willard, physician, capitalist, and philanthropist; Jerome "Brud" Holland, Ambassador to Sweden, Cornell football star, and first African American director of the New York Stock Exchange; and Eliza Wright Osborne, suffragette and a leader in the women's rights movement.

Leon Czolgosz, President William McKinley's assassin, is buried at Soule Cemetery in nearby Sennett. His grave is marked simply, "Fort Hill Remains."

Address 19 Fort Street, Auburn, NY 13021, +1 (315) 253-8132, www.forthillcemetery.net | Getting there From downtown Auburn, take West Genesee Street to Fort Street | Hours Daily sunrise–sunset | Tip In 1889, Julius A. Schweinfurth designed the Bradley Mortuary Chapel at Fort Hill, using a small English country church in Cornwall as a model. The chapel serves as the cemetery office and gatehouse at the Fort Street entrance.

35 Fuertes Observatory

The sky's the limit

A distinguished civil engineer, Estevan A. Fuertes worked on public infrastructure in his native Puerto Rico, on the Croton Aqueduct for New York City, and on early Panama Canal surveys for the US government. He was lured to Cornell in 1873 by Andrew Dickson White, the university's first president, to establish the Department of Civil Engineering. He was instrumental in the development of primitive observatories on the campus, training engineering seniors to measure stars for calculations of time and position. Upon completion of the university's then "state-of-the-art" observatory in 1917, it was named in his honor.

Under the direction of Professor Irving Porter Church, a graduate of Fuertes' early civil engineering program, its main instrument, a 12-inch refracting telescope, driven by a German-made clockwork mechanism, was installed in October 1922.

On clear Friday nights, visitors head up to the Fuertes Observatory for a star-studded evening – a view of the cosmos through the antique telescope. A spiral staircase leads to the observation deck, where undergraduate student members of the Cornell Astronomical Society share historical background, demonstrate the telescope operation, and explain what to look for in different seasons, as the night sky changes throughout the year. The 10-ton dome is rotated into position for its slit to align with a specific portion of the expanse, and visitors take turns viewing planets, stars, and galaxies. Among celestial objects, Jupiter and Saturn are commonly visible, and the telescope can see far enough into space for an occasional view of Pluto.

The observatory is open to the public every Friday evening during the school year, regardless of weather; on cloudy nights, the student guides provide tours of the historic facility, including a small museum room with exhibits and vintage astronomical equipment.

Address 209 Cradit Farm Drive, Ithaca, NY 14850, +1 (607) 255-3557, www.cornellastrosociety.org | **Getting there** Take the Triphammer Road exit from Route 13; follow Triphammer Road to Hanshaw Road, then Pleasant Grove Road to Cradit Farm Drive | **Hours** Fri (Sep–May) 8pm–midnight | **Tip** Cornell's Lab of Ornithology is named for Estevan's son, Louis Agassiz Fuertes, ornithologist and illustrator, considered one of the most prolific American bird artists (159 Sapsucker Woods Road, Ithaca, NY 14850, www.birds.cornell.edu).

36 Gannett Hill "Jump Off"

View from the top

There's arguably one place that provides the best view of the influence of glaciers in sculpting the U-shaped valleys and steepened hillsides of the Finger Lakes region. Its story begins with a man who carved out an empire in America's newspaper world, and who was born in 1876 on a small farm in South Bristol, just west of Canandaigua Lake.

Frank Ernest Gannett peddled papers as a boy and worked his way through Cornell University as a cub reporter for *The Ithaca Journal*. After graduating in 1898, he became the *Journal*'s managing editor, and by 1912, its owner. In 1918, he bought two Rochester newspapers and by the end of the 1920s, owned 15 dailies in New York and other papers in New Jersey, Connecticut, and Illinois. Active in politics, Gannett arrived in Philadelphia with three circus elephants to attend the 1940 Republican Convention, but lost his bid for the presidential nomination to Wendell Willkie.

During his lifetime, Frank Gannett amassed a publishing group of 22 newspapers in 18 cities. He owned four radio stations and three television stations. Today, the company is the country's largest newspaper group, with 95 daily newspapers, including national publication *USA Today*.

Established in 1926 by Ontario County, one of the oldest county parks in New York State was named to honor the extraordinary life of Frank Gannett, and one of the park's most striking features is the view from Gannett Hill. Follow the Bristol Hills Trail from the west parking area to reach the "Jump Off," the highest point in the county at 2,256 feet.

The lookout deck provides panoramic views of the rolling hills, valleys, and forests that stretch out across the region. On clear days, it's possible to see all the way to Seneca and Cayuga Lakes to the east, and the most magical time to visit is in fall, when the vibrant colors of orange, yellow, red, and purple adorn the landscape.

Address 6475 Gannett Hill Park Drive, Naples, NY 14512, +1 (585) 374-6250, www.ontariocountyny.gov | Getting there From Naples, follow Route 21S to Bristol Springs Road, turn onto Rhine Street (becomes South Gannett Hill Road), and continue to Gannett Hill Park Drive | Hours Daily 9am–9pm | Tip The geography and topography of Elmira's Harris Hill not only create extraordinary conditions for gliding enthusiasts, but provide one of the most dramatic overlooks in the region, 700 feet above the Chemung River Valley (391 Harris Hill Road, Elmira, NY 14903).

37_Genesee Beer Sign

View to a brew

When does a commercial advertisement become a cultural icon? In 1952, the Genesee Brewing Company of Rochester installed the giant (and hard to miss) sign, measuring 26 feet high and 48 feet wide, atop the Speno Music building, illuminating the city skyline in neon letters. Standing 85 feet from the ground to the top, the sign became a familiar fixture of downtown Auburn.

It was a sweet deal for Nicholas Speno Jr., owner of the music store. The brewing company not only paid an annual rent of $1,500, but the contract included a case of Genny Cream Ale, his favorite brewski, delivered to Speno each month.

In 1975, the sign went dark, as an energy crisis drove up the cost of powering the neon tubing. The tubes were removed, and the letters painted in Genesee's signature red and white. By 2008, the fate of the sign, then showing its age, was in doubt when it appeared that Genesee might stop paying rent. By then, the sign had become an irreplaceable part of the city's heritage, and the Speno family worked with the Auburn Business Improvement District to raise awareness about its significance. Not only did the effort convince folks the sign was a local treasure that needed to be protected, the message was heard loud and clear at Genesee headquarters.

In 2011, brewery management teamed up with local business leaders to invest $60,000, retrofitting new wiring and 9,120 state-of-the-art LED lights, and restoring the sign to its former glory. On August 13, 2011, thousands of citizens crowded the area in front of the building to celebrate the re-lighting after decades of darkness. Today, the Genesee Beer sign is illuminated on a timer, automatically turning on at dusk and turning off at dawn. The beloved sign, a commercial display that became an essential visual landmark, continues to greet motorists driving through downtown Auburn, inspiring thirst in all who pass.

Address 3 East Genesee Street, Auburn, NY 13021, www.geneseebeer.com | Getting there From North Street/South Street (Route 38), turn onto East Genesee Street | Hours Unrestricted | Tip In 1933, a group of local students planted 260 pine trees spelling out each letter of their town's name, "Canisteo," on a 90-foot by 300-foot patch of hillside. According to Ripley's Believe It or Not!, it's "The World's Largest Living Sign" (Cemetery Road, Canisteo, NY 14456, www.villageofcanisteo.com).

38 Geneva on the Lake

A repurposed monastery

The glory of the Italian Renaissance comes to life in the Italian city of Frascati, about 12 miles from Rome, and also in the Finger Lakes city of Geneva, about 4,000 miles from Rome.

The chief attractions in Frascati are the stately villas built by popes, cardinals and Roman nobility, with beautiful gardens and fountains. It was Villa Lancellotti, constructed in 1582 by Cardinal Bonanni, that caught the attention of Byron Nester on his visit to Italy. After inheriting the fortune his father had amassed from processing barley into malt for the brewing industry, Nester commissioned the design and construction of a grand mansion just south of Geneva, drawing inspiration from the grandeur of Villa Lancellotti. The imposing structure was built in 1910 with brick and concrete block and coated in stucco, its interior appointed with Italian marble fireplaces, tapestries, Ionic columns, and wood-coffered ceilings.

The mansion remained home to the Nester family until 1946, when it was purchased by the Capuchin Fathers, a religious order of Franciscan friars of the Catholic Church, who operated the Immaculate Heart of Mary Seminary on the property for two decades. Later abandoned for several years, the estate was transformed into a boutique resort in 1981, and the manicured gardens, originally designed by the Rochester firm of Pitkin and Weinrichter in 1930, were meticulously restored to their former splendor.

Situated on a 10-acre bluff with sweeping views of Seneca Lake, the garden is open to both guests and the public. Come and stroll through the lush, rolling landscape with symmetrical hedges, colorful flower beds, a pool appointed with terracotta urns, and Adirondack chairs at the lakeside. Classical sculptures of Greek goddesses adorn the colonnade. A stone grotto dedicated to Saint Anne and sculptures depicting the Crucifixion hint at the estate's storied past.

Address 1001 Lochland Road (Route 14), Geneva, NY 14456, +1 (315) 789-7190, www.genevaonthelake.com | Getting there Follow Route 14 south from the city of Geneva | Hours Daily 11am–3pm | Tip Nearby Geneva Hall, built in 1822, is the first building of Hobart and William Smith College, and the oldest standing academic building in Western New York (648 South Main Street, Geneva, NY 14456, www.hws.edu).

39 Gideon Granger Homestead

Deliver de letter, de sooner de better

A Yale-educated lawyer, Gideon Granger, made an unsuccessful bid for Congress in 1798, yet he caught the attention of President Thomas Jefferson because of his essays in support of Jefferson's political views. In 1802, Granger was appointed Postmaster General in the president's cabinet, a position he held until 1814, making him the longest-serving Postmaster General in US history.

In 1803, the Louisiana Purchase extended US sovereignty beyond the Mississippi River, nearly doubling the nation's size, and Granger's job included establishing a postal service to the new settlements. Although he earned widespread admiration during his time for strengthening the early Federal Post Office Department, Granger is unfortunately now remembered for persuading Congress to pass a national ban, prohibiting African Americans from carrying the mail.

Upon leaving the cabinet in 1814, Granger moved to Canandaigua with his wife Mindwell, where he built a home that he predicted would be "unrivaled in all the nation." The three-story Federal-style mansion, inspired by the works of the distinguished British architect Robert Adam, took two years to build and, upon completion in 1816, exceeded expectations.

Four generations of the Granger family occupied this imposing mansion, now a museum, where an expert guide takes you on a walk through the home, highlighting architectural details and original furnishings. The north parlor displays portraits of Gideon and Mindwell, and the south parlor includes Mindwell's lolling chair and footstool, set near the fireplace. The parlors hosted many distinguished visitors over the years, including Edwin Everett, Charles Dickens, and Phillips Brooks. For 30 years, from 1876 to 1906, the Granger Place School, a "finishing school" for young ladies, occupied the homestead.

Address 295 North Main Street, Canandaigua, NY 14424, +1 (585) 394-1472, www.grangerhomestead.org | **Getting there** From Route 20, drive into downtown Canandaigua on South Main Street to North Main Street | **Hours** May–Oct Wed–Sun 11am–4pm | **Tip** On the grounds of the estate, a Carriage Museum includes a collection of over 80 horse-drawn carriages, carts, wagons, sleighs, and sleds dating back to the early 1800s (295 North Main Street, Canandaigua, NY 14424).

40 Gillette Skirt Company

Based on a true story

Noah Horace Gillette first started producing made-to-order petticoats on the second floor of a building on Clinton Avenue in Cortland in 1896. His Gillette Skirt Company moved to Homer Avenue before constructing the city's first concrete block building on Miller Street in 1905. That year, Chester Ellsworth Gillette took a position at his uncle's factory, where he met seamstress Grace Brown, and the two began a romantic and sexual relationship. At the same time, Gillette moved up the social rung and began dating the daughter of a wealthy family.

In the spring of 1906, Brown revealed she was pregnant and urged Gillette to marry her, complicating Gillette's pursuit of the upper-class girl. Despite the tension, the couple planned a summer trip to Big Moose Lake in Herkimer County. On July 11, Gillette took Brown out on the lake in a rowboat, where he struck her with a tennis racquet and left her to drown. Gillette was charged with her murder, and the subsequent trial – the O. J. Simpson trial of its day – sparked a media frenzy, making headlines around the world. He was found guilty, and, on March 30, 1908, executed by electric chair at Auburn Prison.

The story became the basis of Theodore Dreiser's *An American Tragedy,* named by *Time* magazine as one the top 100 novels written in English since 1923 (the novel was banned in Boston in 1927 and burned by the Nazis in Germany in 1933 because it "deals with low love affairs"). The novel inspired the 1951 film *A Place in the Sun* with Montgomery Clift and Shelly Winters as the tragic couple, and Elizabeth Taylor as the rich girl.

The former Gillette Skirt Company building stands mostly forgotten at the edge of town, the once-bustling structure now silent, its windows covered, its imposing brick walls grim, as if time has stopped, but the memory of its connection to the tragic murder has not.

Address 32 Miller Street (at Stockton Place), Cortland, NY 13045 | Getting there From Clinton Avenue (Route 13), turn onto North Main Street, then onto Miller Street | Hours Unrestricted | Tip Born just outside Cortland, Amelia Bloomer is remembered for her fashion statement linked to the women's suffrage movement. A pair of the historic bloomers can be seen on display at the nearby Cortland County Historical Society (25 Homer Avenue, Cortland, NY 13045, www.cortlandhistory.org).

41 Glenhaven Farm

Master class in blueberry picking

For over four decades, John Tamburello has been perfecting the art of growing blueberries. The story began with John's purchase of an idyllic and historic farm property, a dream supported by his close-knit Italian family. A graduate of the Ag School at Cornell, he was on a path to become a fruit grower, and in 1979, that dream ripened into a U-pick blueberry farm.

By 1985, with 6,000 plants flourishing on 11 acres of the estate, Glenhaven Farm's harvest was sizable enough for John to join the Ithaca Farmers Market, introducing local shoppers to plump, sweet, organically grown fruit sold by the pint. His mainstay Northern highbush variety, "Bluecrop," was selected to yield large, bright blueberries by mid-summer, and a smaller yield of late-ripening, slightly tart "Elliots" extended offerings into September.

Every summer, John welcomes hundreds of folks who, in cherished tradition, come to pick their own berries straight from the bushes. Follow roadside signs to the farm, drive to the barn, where you pick up a six-quart container, or two if you're more ambitious, then to the parking area. The lush blueberry field is just ahead, and you're ready to start picking. The best ones are deep blue or blue-black in color with a silver or grayish sheen (bloom). Pick one and taste it. A burst of sweetness and a hint of tartness melts on your tongue – a taste of summer.

Most folks will spend an hour and a half to two hours in the field before heading back to the barn to weigh their harvest, pay for their bounty, and maybe linger for a wine tasting. At the end of each season, John reserves a portion of fruit to produce small batches of blueberry wine, aged in the cellar of his 1873 farmhouse, ready for sale by the following summer. After a satisfying day, with hands slightly stained from the juicy berries and baskets brimming, it's time to head home.

Address 6121 Sirrine Road, Trumansburg, NY 14886, +1 (607) 387-9031, www.glenhavenfarm.com | Getting there From Route 96 (West Main Street) in Trumansburg, follow Route 227 (Hector Street) to Sirrine Road | Hours Jul–Sep daily 8am–5pm | Tip Established in 1973, the Ithaca Farmers Market at Steamboat Landing is a nationally known cooperative of members who grow or produce fresh, local, and sustainable goods, including fruits, vegetables, meats, cheeses, baked goods, and artisan crafts (545 3rd Street, Ithaca, NY 14850, www.ithacamarket.com).

42 Glenn H. Curtiss Museum

America's first "flyboy"

Most people know about the Wright Brothers, yet there's a far more interesting character in the story of early aviation. The very first air show in America was held in Hammondsport on July 4, 1908, when native son Glenn H. Curtiss, holder of Pilot's License No. 1, motored an aircraft called the "June Bug" and rose 20 feet off the ground, flying the craft for 5,090 feet to the cheers of hundreds of spectators. The next year, he flew the "Golden Flyer" a distance of 24.7 miles to establish a world distance record.

Born in 1878, Curtiss' first love was the bicycle. As a young man he worked as a Western Union bicycle messenger before starting his own bicycle shop. By his twenties he had begun building motorcycles, and powered by a 4.4-liter V-8 engine, in 1907, he set a speed record of 136 miles per hour – at the time, faster than anything on land, sea, or in the air. Newspapers called him the "Fastest Man on Earth," locals called him "Hellrider." After turning his attention to planes, Curtiss went on to make countless contributions to the field of aviation, among them building 6,800 "Jennys," first used as World War I Air Service trainers, then as barnstormers and mail-carrying airplanes.

The Glenn H. Curtiss Museum is home to priceless artifacts and exhibits, including vintage and restored bicycles and motorcycles, and more than two dozen authentic or reproduction, full-size aircraft. On display are replicas of the record-setting cycle; the historic "June Bug" (only the original propeller survives); A-1 Triad, the first amphibious aircraft; and an authentic "Jenny." Unlike many museums, you can get up close and personal to the legendary collections. Don't miss the chance to visit the Restoration Shop, where the Curtiss P-40 Warhawk is being recreated from vintage and fabricated parts, and you can talk with volunteer craftsmen.

Address 8419 Route 54, Hammondsport, NY 14840, +1 (607) 569-2160, www.glennhcurtissmuseum.org | Getting there Follow Route 54 south of the village for 1 mile | Hours May–Oct daily 9am–5pm, Nov–Apr daily 10am–4pm; guided tours available, and also self-guided tours so you can visit at your own pace (check the website for how to book) | Tip After a visit to the museum, take a ride along Keuka Lake to Point of the Bluff Vineyards, where you can whet your whistle with a four-pack of Hangar 17 wine. Every purchase supports the Curtiss Museum (10489 County Route 76, Hammondsport, NY 14840, www.pointofthebluffvineyards.com).

43 Gourdlandia

Ithaca is gourd-geous

Gourds are nature's quirky little sculptures with an almost magical appeal, and they have inspired humans for thousands of years. They come in unique shapes, colors, and varieties, which makes them natural "canvases" for human creativity, as imaginative handcrafters hollow-out, carve, paint, and embellish them in countless ways, as both functional objects and works of art.

The name Gourdlandia conjures an enchanting place dedicated to all things gourd-related, where gourds, bursting with personality and humor, are celebrated. Gourdlandia is indeed such a place: a garden, a workshop, and a small store selling all manner of creations that emerge from gourds, from lamps to vases, nightlights to necklaces. The first indication that something special is going on here is a 12-foot-tall, gourd-shaped trellis out front, with gourd vines growing over the blacksmith-crafted framework. Step inside the cozy cottage. The vibe is rustic and artistic, with meticulously detailed, decorative pieces displayed on shelves and hanging from the ceiling. Welcome to the weird, wild, wacky world of gourds.

You'll be greeted by the gourdsmith herself, Graham Ottoson, dressed in overalls. After a career as a practicing midwife, Graham, who claims she was always a "dabbler," began transforming these non-edible fruits into objects she believes reflect the deep connection between humans and nature.

Her workspace includes a cluttered table, strewn with a gourd saw and assorted rotary tools – a place for cleaning and scraping, staining and waxing, designing and carving. She often pauses to tell the story of each piece, how she sees the unique shape of each gourd as something playful or profound. It's also a place where she teaches classes. Folks who learn what she does come from all parts of the country to watch a demonstration, learn about the process, and make a piece of gourd art to take home.

Address 77 Rachel Carson Way, Ithaca, NY 14850, +1 (607) 277-0589, www.gourdlandia.com | Getting there From downtown Ithaca, take Route 79 (Mecklenburg Road) to Rachel Carson Way | Hours Mon 9am–1pm, Fri & Sat 1–5pm, or by appointment | Tip Gourdlandia is located in EcoVillage, a model cohousing community based on sustainable systems of living, with 100 homes on 170 acres and a variety of working farms, community gardens, meadows, ponds, and woodlands (100 Rachel Carson Way, Ithaca, NY 14850, www.ecovillageithaca.org).

44 The Grottos of Conesus

The secret of Saint Michael's Mission

In 1872, Bernard J. McQuaid, Catholic bishop of the Rochester diocese, established a vineyard and winery on the west slope of Hemlock Lake to make sacramental wine for his churches. He chose the name O-Neh-Da for his enterprise to respect the native Seneca name for the lake.

Saint Michael's Mission was established in 1926 when the priests and brothers of the Divine Word Missionaries came here to work in the vineyards, and by 1936, the mission had grown to become a seminary school where young men lived, prayed, and studied, while the Sisters of St. Francis provided cooking and laundry services for the community. But times changed, and by 1965 the society decided to move all students to other locations. Only a few retired priests and brothers remained at the mission, which was used briefly for church retreats.

Today, while much of the sprawling complex is vacant, a nearby secluded vale holds a remarkable secret. During his time at the mission, Friar Fridolin Iten created a series of grottos meant for contemplation and private prayer. Over the years, nature reclaimed the area, leaving the stone caves in partial ruins and remnants, and to reach them, you'll need to trek down into the ravine and along uneven terrain. Closest to the mission, the Rosary Grotto is a multi-room stone structure, its walls picturing biblical themes. Further along the wooded grounds, past a collapsed stone bridge and burial markers, you'll see monuments, each making a Station of the Cross. The striking Grotto of the Agony, built into the hillside, holds a large crucifix on the outside, but sadly, the inside is crumbling.

In 1985, the Diocese of Rochester removed statues and religious artifacts from the grottos, but there is enough left to imagine Friar Fridolin Iten's original masterworks. These extraordinary structures, although derelict with time, enchant everyone who ventures here.

Address 5604 Mission Road, Conesus, NY 14435, +1 (585) 310-1803, www.dorchurches.com/stmichaelmission | Getting there From Rochester, take Route 390 to Route 20A, continue to Route 15A South, then Kellogg Road to Marrowback Road; take a right onto Bishop Road, then a left onto Mission Road | Hours By appointment only | Tip A modern shrine, called the Grotto of the Pieta, was built by John Landino on his Wayland homestead in 2018. Spanning 37 feet in width and weighing 125 tons, the grotto includes a statue of Mother Mary cradling Jesus after the crucifixion (11763 Route 38 (Rowe Road), Wayland, NY 14572).

45 Hammerstone School

Women teaching women to build stuff

Nestled in an old barn amidst the rolling hills of Trumansburg, Hammerstone is one of the country's only all-female carpentry schools. Surrounded by apple orchards and clucking chickens, hands-on workshops are taught by women for women, fostering a supportive space for prospects to enter the male-dominated trades.

A feminist fairytale, the Hammerstone School was the brainchild of Maria Klemperer-Johnson. Although she started along the path to a PhD in geology at Cornell, a passion for carpentry drove her to leave studies behind and pursue a career in woodcraft. After collaborating on a project with Liz Coakley, the two craftswomen launched Hammerstone.

Since its beginning in 2013, the school has expanded its staff and curriculum. All the way from Adirondack chairs to tiny houses, aspiring female carpenters learn to construct almost anything at the picturesque workshop. Whether embarking on home renovations or dipping a toe in the carpentry pool, the school serves as a resource for women who are determined to build. The popular two-day basic carpentry class warms up beginners with the fundamental tools of the trade, measuring and marking, using hand- and circular-saws, assembly with screws and nails, and understanding wood as a material. Since courses are offered at sliding-scale tuition rates, the school fulfills a mission of increasing accessibility for all who wish to enter the trades.

While joining the construction world once felt like a towering feat for gender minorities, Hammerstone makes it possible for students to overcome the challenges of the profession. Courses for non-binary learners are offered, while collaboration with Open Doors English and the Youth Farm Project has increased Hammerstone's reach. The scenic campus disguises an innovative feminist workshop. Within its rustic walls, creative projects are reshaping the landscape of gender equality.

Address 3285 Jacksonville Road, Trumansburg, NY 14886, +1 (607) 280-8513, www.hammerstoneschool.com | Getting there Follow Trumansburg Road north out of Ithaca, turn left on Perry City Road, then left again onto Jacksonville Road | Hours By appointment only | Tip A second location of the Hammerstone School in Ithaca's West End provides students with accessibility to transit, and the heated space allows teachers to expand programs throughout the entire year (720 West Green Street, Ithaca, NY 14850).

46 Hangar Theatre

Amelia Earhart landed here

In another life, the site of Ithaca's Hangar Theatre served as Ithaca Municipal Airport, only the third airport in the United States. Built in 1916 with two sod airstrips cut through a peach orchard, the airport was used by the Thomas-Morse Aviation Company for the testing of early airplanes and as an aviation school before, during, and after World War I. Its proximity to Cayuga Lake permitted experiments with flying boats and hydroplanes.

During the Depression, a Civil Works Administration project expanded the airport with asphalt runways and a two-story glass, steel, and cinder-block hangar. On November 2, 1935, Amelia Earhart landed her plane at the airport, invited by Cornell University to talk about the experience of her transatlantic flight. "My flight," she explained, "added little to aviation, as literally hundreds of people have already made the trip by air in airplanes or lighter-than-air craft. But I do hope that it interested women in aviation."

During World War II, over 4,000 pilots were trained here, but eventually the short runways, lake marshes on the north side, and fog in the lake valley posed limits to growth, and in 1948, Cornell and the city opened the Ithaca-Tompkins Regional Airport on university-owned land near East Hill, transferring ownership of the property and hangar to the county in 1956. With a grant from New York governor and philanthropist Nelson Rockefeller, the abandoned hangar was renovated in 1975, re-designed by architect Robert Manning, and converted into a cultural hub for the city. The inaugural season of the Hangar Theatre opened with a production of *Man of La Mancha*.

The 364-seat theater currently offers a diverse array of plays, musicals, and concerts. On a visit here, you'll see lobby walls with the names of the volunteer corps and the historic photo of Amelia Earhart upon her arrival at the old airport.

Address 801 Taughannock Boulevard, Ithaca, NY 14850, +1 (607) 273-2787 (box office), +1 (607) 273-8588 (business office), www.hangartheatre.org | Getting there Follow Taughannock Boulevard (Route 96) north, just over a mile from downtown Ithaca | Hours Visit website for performance details | Tip The S-4 Scout, built by the Thomas Morse Airplane Company in Ithaca, nicknamed the "Tommy" plane, was used to train American pilots during World War I. An original, fully restored "Tommy" is on display at the downtown History Center (110 North Tioga Street, Ithaca, NY 14850, www.thehistorycenter.net).

47 Harriet Tubman Home

Heroine of Black history

Born into slavery in Dorchester County, Maryland, Harriet Tubman escaped to freedom in the North in 1849 to become the most famous "conductor" on the Underground Railroad, leading enslaved people to freedom before the Civil War. With savings from her work as a nurse, cook, and lecturer, as well as a small pension she received for her service during the war, she was able to purchase a farmhouse at 182 South Street in Auburn. Tubman lived in Auburn from 1859 until her passing in 1913, and the city has deeply embraced her legacy. Although her life story was told in a 2019 motion picture, a visit to Auburn provides a deeper and more profound understanding of her remarkable life.

The Tubman Home, including a display of her personal artifacts, was designated a National Historic Landmark in 1974 and added to the National Register of Historic Places in 1999. Guides offer detailed tours of Tubman's home and property, quite literally following in her footsteps.

A short distance from the home, the city celebrates her legacy with a 26-foot by 61-foot mural by local architect and artist Arthur Hutchinson, commanding attention at the corner of Genesee and North Streets. The theme includes scenes of Tubman at various stages of her life, including her as a nurse during the Civil War, a participant in the women's suffrage movement, and as an older woman in the apple orchard she cultivated at her home.

What most powerfully brings Harriet Tubman to life here is a striking seven-and-a-half-foot-tall bronze statue by sculptor Brian P. Hanlon on the terrace of the Equal Rights Heritage Center. It represents a young Harriet, traveling on the Underground Railroad, clothed in a shawl, jacket, and pleated skirt. She strides forward, extending her left hand behind her as if signaling to a group to follow. In her right hand, she holds the ring of a lantern, illuminating the pathway to freedom.

Address 180 South Street (Route 34), Auburn, NY 13021, +1 (315) 252-2081, www.harriettubmanhome.com | **Getting there** From downtown Auburn, follow South Street to the corner of Danforth Avenue | **Hours** Tue–Sat 10am–4pm (tours 10am and 2pm) | **Tip** Built in 1891, the Thompson Memorial African Methodist Episcopal Zion Church was called the "Freedom Church." In addition to the membership of Harriet Tubman, the church served as a place of worship for Frederick Douglass and Sojourner Truth (49 Parker Street, Auburn NY 13021).

48 Harrisburg Hollow Steeple

Soul survivor

During the 19th century, as religious movements took hold in the Finger Lakes, Methodism gained widespread popularity among common folks for its simplified doctrines, spiritual preaching, and emphasis on a more personal connection with faith rather than ritualistic forms of worship. From their earliest history, Methodists planted churches in even the smallest communities and remote areas, often underserved by other religious institutions. One of those churches was built in 1891 at the intersection of Harrisburg Hollow Road and Robbins Road between Bath and Wheeler.

The Harrisburg Hollow Methodist Church served generations of the surrounding rural community until 1943, when a shrinking congregation found it easier to attend larger, more centralized churches in nearby Bath and Corning. The wooden structure stood abandoned for decades, and it began to weaken, battered by the elements of time and weather. The roof sagged, the walls bowed, and eventually, the main body of the church collapsed and was removed, but the church's steeple – the tallest part of the structure – continued to stand defiantly upright.

Though most of the church is gone, the free-standing spire remains as a silent, symbolic monument, a reminder of the past weddings, baptisms, and holiday services once held here over the years. Local folks lovingly tend this roadside wonder, restored in 1983, repainted and reshingled in 2004. Recently, a park bench was added to the grounds, enhancing the setting and offering a peaceful spot for reflection. Today, the steeple towers over the surrounding landscape at this quiet corner, delighting back-road drivers who come upon it unexpectedly.

But don't pass by without stopping. Open the red door, walk inside, and you'll see a small pew facing a modest communion table with a Bible. The steeple has been transformed into a miniature church.

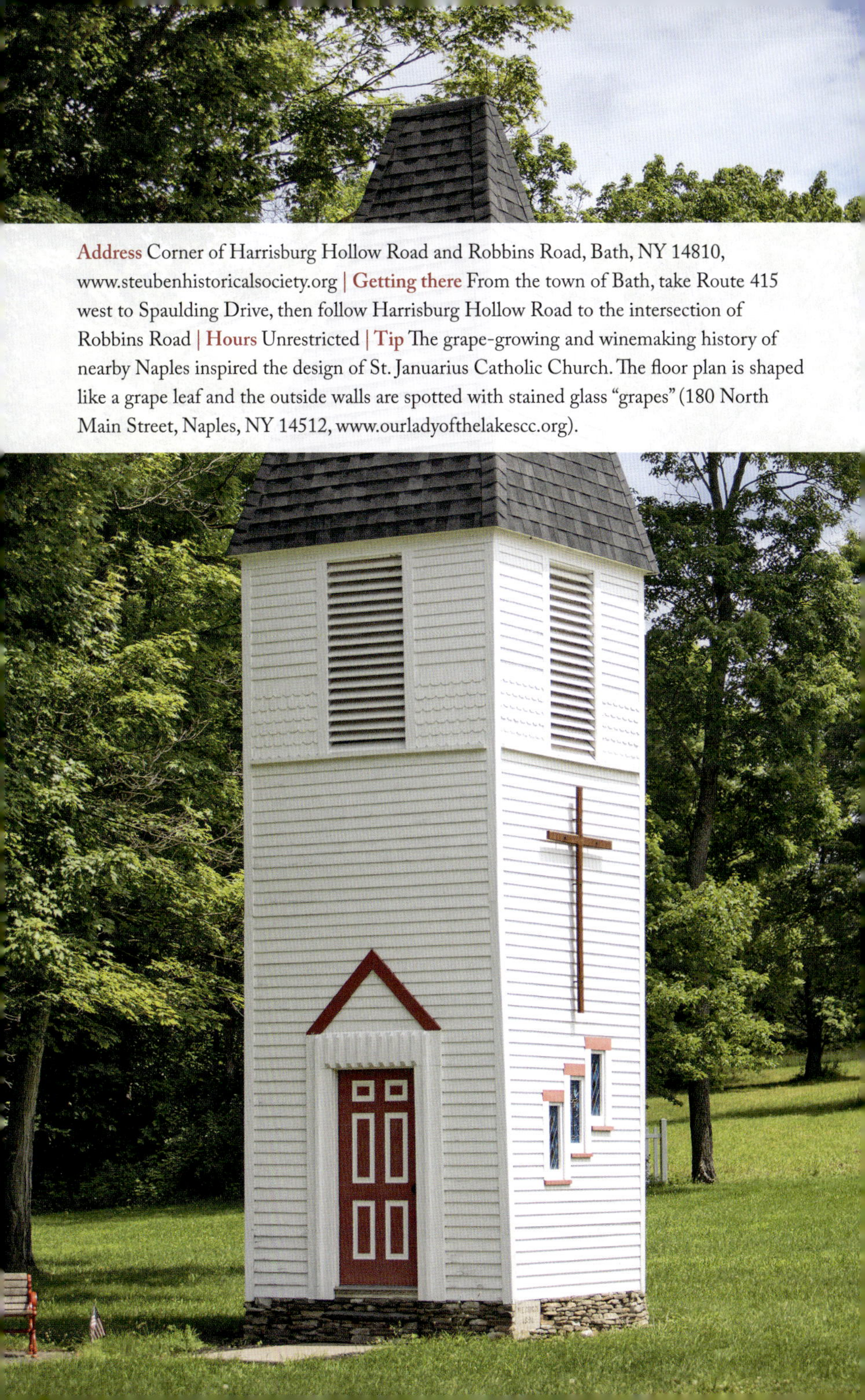

Address Corner of Harrisburg Hollow Road and Robbins Road, Bath, NY 14810, www.steubenhistoricalsociety.org | **Getting there** From the town of Bath, take Route 415 west to Spaulding Drive, then follow Harrisburg Hollow Road to the intersection of Robbins Road | **Hours** Unrestricted | **Tip** The grape-growing and winemaking history of nearby Naples inspired the design of St. Januarius Catholic Church. The floor plan is shaped like a grape leaf and the outside walls are spotted with stained glass "grapes" (180 North Main Street, Naples, NY 14512, www.ourladyofthelakescc.org).

49 Howland Stone Store

Socially conscious commerce model

The Quakers, also known as the Religious Society of Friends, were drawn to this region by its fertile land and abundant opportunities for agriculture. They established a community here in the early 19th century, centered around their religious beliefs and values. The Howland family, descended from Henry Howland of the Mayflower Howlands, arrived in Sherwood, where Slocum Howland built his general store in 1837.

A Quaker, abolitionist, prohibitionist, and suffragist, Slocum became a successful entrepreneur, dabbling in commodities and railroad stocks. The store became the center of his diversified business interests, where he leveraged his commercial network to help escaped slaves reach Canada and actively advocated for social reforms.

The sturdy, enduring cobblestone store is now a heritage museum, highlighting the Howland family's contributions to progressive movements into the 20th century, especially abolition and women's suffrage. The main floor displays original goods, tools, and household wares that would have been sold during that time. There's a grandfather clock, a vintage checkerboard, a giant map of the Underground Railroad, books from the village's first library (including a signed copy of Booker T. Washington's *Up from Slavery*), and a handsome portrait of Slocum himself.

You think you might have seen everything – until you walk upstairs. The room is filled with "cabinets of curiosities," hundreds of meticulously documented artifacts and souvenirs from the Howland family's world travels. There are shells from the Nile River and stones from the Sahara Desert, Bedouin jewelry, communion bread from a Coptic Church, mastodon teeth from who-knows-where, Mexican pottery, a chunk of marble from the Temple of Zeus in Olympia, and a remnant of wood from the home of George Fox, founder of the Quakers, from Leicestershire, England, just to name a few.

Address 2956 Route 34B, Sherwood, NY 13026, +1 (315) 303-2145, www.howlandstonestore.org | Getting there From Ithaca, follow Route 34 to Route 34B; from Auburn, follow Route 34 to Route 34B | Hours Sat & Sun 1–4pm (May–Oct or by appointment) | Tip Slocum's granddaughter, Isabel, rebuilt a house three doors away and called it "Opendore." The second floor is filled with posters, banners, memorabilia supporting the 19th amendment, and a slice of Susan B. Anthony's birthday cake (2978 Route 34B, Sherwood, NY 13026).

50 Ithaca Gun Smokestack

Annie get your gun

The Ithaca Gun factory was established in 1883 on a slope that became known as Gun Hill, where a nearby waterfall supplied the plant's main source of energy. Today, while the sprawling factory is gone, its giant 150-foot brick smokestack, towering above the Fall Creek neighborhood, serves as a city landmark and a reminder of Ithaca Gun Company's remarkable history.

In its early years, Ithaca Gun was responsible for much of the early industry here, producing side-by-side double-barreled shotguns with engravings on the metal parts and elaborately carved wooden gunstocks. One of the company's early customers, Annie Oakley, the legendary sharpshooter who performed in *Buffalo Bill Cody's Wild West* traveling shows, used Ithaca guns during her performances. In 1909, Teddy Roosevelt carried Ithaca guns on a year-long hunting trip to Africa. And John Philip Sousa, famous composer, conductor, and leader of the Marine Band, was also an accomplished trap shooter who owned several Ithaca guns.

But it was with the company's Model 37, introduced in 1937, that Ithaca Gun truly carved out a place in popular culture. Ernest Hemingway, author and adventurer, carried a Model 37 during his hunting expeditions. President Dwight D. Eisenhower used an Ithaca Model 37 during his frequent hunting trips. Other notable owners of the reliable shotgun included Clark Gable, John Wayne, Roy Rogers, and Ted Williams. Chuck Connors, the actor best known for his role as Lucas McCain in the television series *The Rifleman*, used an Ithaca Model 37 in the show.

Ithaca Gun sustained itself through sales of the Model 37 and various other products to the US government and law-enforcement agencies, yet following a series of bankruptcies, the factory overlooking Ithaca Falls was finally shut down and the factory demolished, leaving only the towering stack, a lone sentinel.

Address Lake Street, Ithaca, NY 14853 | **Getting there** From downtown Ithaca, follow Route 13 N, take the Stewart Park/Auburn exit and turn right at the stop sign; follow Route 34 (becomes Lake Street) – you'll be able to view the smokestack on the left | **Hours** Unrestricted | **Tip** Visit the History Center exhibit highlighting the Ithaca Gun Company as well as many other examples of Tompkins County's rich industrial history (110 North Tioga Street, Ithaca, NY 14850, www.thehistorycenter.net).

51 Jennings Department Store

Small-town shopping since 1860

By the time Richard Sears and Alvah Roebuck opened their first department store in Chicago in 1892, Henry Jennings had already been serving folks in Moravia for 32 years. One of the oldest continuously operating retail stores in America, the Jennings Department Store, established in 1860, has survived the Civil War, the Great Depression, two World Wars, and two pandemics, defying the odds and remaining a reliable cornerstone of the community in an era dominated by malls and online shopping.

Thousands of locals have worked here, shopped here, and created memories. There were special-occasion dresses for women, fedoras and Oxfords for men, and wooden toys for kids. In the 1930s, many bought their first radio at Jennings.

Henry Jennings began by offering a variety of goods under one roof – uncommon for the time. In 1921, after Henry had been running the place for more than 60 years, his son, Charles, entered into a partnership with his father in 1888. An expert in fitting and repairing footwear, Charles became known as "The Shoe Man," and it's been said that no matter what shoes you came in for, you left with the shoes he wanted you to buy. Charles' son Carlton worked in the store on and off from the 1920s to the '50s, taking on "Bucky" Smith to manage things during his frequent travels.

In 1979, the store was sold to Claude Stoker, a long-standing employee, and on his retirement in 2003, ownership passed to his daughter, Lynette, and her husband, Mark Wood. Under their stewardship, Jennings has adapted to practical retail needs. Walking through the store today, visitors are greeted by rows of sturdy footwear and work boots, outdoor gear, and rugged Carhartt clothing. Timeless charm is preserved with well-worn wooden floors and vintage-style displays. Look around and you'll see Henry's original safe, a 1914 cash register, and vintage photographs, frozen in time.

Address 147 Main Street, Moravia, NY 13118, +1 (315) 497-1341 | Getting there From Auburn, follow Route 38 (west Lake Road) into Moravia; turn right onto Main Street | Hours Mon–Fri 9am–6pm, Sat 9am–5pm, Sun 11am–4pm | Tip Nearby St. Matthew's, an Episcopal church where President Millard Fillmore was married, is adorned with 18 oak statues from Hans Meyer's workshop in Germany. Other hand carvings surrounding the altar include panels, a lectern, and a baptismal font, crafted by Charles S. Hall of the Roycroft Arts and Craft Community (14 Church Street, Moravia, NY 13118).

52 John Quincy Howe House

Home of the only two-story outhouse

Listed on the National Register of Historic Places, the grand mansion of Dr. John Quincy Howe was donated to the Phelps Community Historical Society and now functions as a museum with an array of exhibits that capture and narrate the rich history of Phelps. Built in 1869 in the distinctive French Empire Style, with elements that include a slate mansard roof, dormers with elaborate surrounds, and symmetrical façade, the home has been lovingly restored to its original grandeur. Visitors can walk through the rooms, admire the architecture, and learn about the history of the house and its inhabitants, yet most are drawn here because of a unique and intriguing feature.

The construction of the Erie Canal, completed in 1825, created immense opportunities for land speculation, and astute individuals made fortunes by buying and selling properties near the canal. Dr. John Quincy Howe was one of those individuals, and people with money often have the freedom to be eccentric. Besides the lavish details of his home's interior, the Howe home was built with a two-story, double-decker privy, situated in a brick, tower-like part of the building, thought to be the only structure of its kind anywhere in the United States.

In another rarity, there is a "three-holer" at each level, differently-sized holes for men, women, and children. Access to "the best seat in the house" could be gained from both the first and second floors. The upper level of the outhouse was accessible from the family quarters on the second floor, while the lower level served household staff on the ground floor, a design intended to accommodate both the family and their servants while maintaining separate spaces.

With the installation of plumbed flush toilets, the family no longer used the second-floor privy, while the staff continued to use the first-floor facility from their quarters.

Address 66 Main Street, Phelps, NY 14532, +1 (315) 548 4940, www.phelpsnyhistory.com | Getting there From the New York Thruway (I-90), take Interchange 42 into Phelps | Hours Wed–Fri 10am–4pm (or by appointment) | Tip The long, communal trough urinal system at Schoellkopf Field, Cornell University's football stadium, is located in the men's restrooms under the stands, and designed to accommodate dozens of users at once (513 Campus Road, Cornell University, Ithaca, NY 14850).

53 Johnson Museum of Art

Convergence of art and architecture

In 1886, Samuel Curtis Johnson formulated a product to care for parquet floors, and 87 years later, his grandson, Herbert Fisk Johnson Jr., became the primary benefactor of this art museum perched atop a 1,000-foot slope on the Cornell University campus, a site that founder Ezra Cornell originally intended to remain free of any buildings. The location, known as "Library Slope," with a sweeping panorama of Cayuga Lake and the surrounding area, was the very spot where Cornell stood when he announced his intention to found the university.

Despite Ezra's wish, architect I. M. Pei, whose masterpieces include the Louvre Pyramid and the J. F. K. Library, called his desire to build on the hallowed ground "an obsession." The decision was controversial, but Pei designed the structure to harmonize with the landscape and preserve the surrounding views. While the museum's permanent collection includes significant works by artists such as Rembrandt, Francisco Goya, Henri Matisse, Pablo Picasso, Andy Warhol, Georgia O'Keeffe, Thomas Cole, and Winslow Homer, the building's innovative design is an iconic piece of art itself.

Pei conducted extensive research on local materials to create a specialized blend of concrete, incorporating sand and small coarse stone aggregate. This mix was then poured into a framework of boards and panels, which helped shape the structure, and added a unique texture to the surface. The building is punctuated by long horizontal bands of windows that sweep across the upper floors, flooding the galleries with natural light and complementing the artwork on display. The fifth floor, where the structure dramatically juts out over the open-air sculpture garden, makes a visual connection between indoor and outdoor environments.

The elegant design seamlessly blends art and architecture, making the building an integral part of the museum experience.

Address 114 Central Avenue, Ithaca, NY 14853, +1 (607) 255-6464, www.museum.cornell.edu | **Getting there** From University Avenue on Cornell campus, turn onto Central Avenue | **Hours** Tue–Sun 10am–5pm (Wed–Sun 11am–4pm during summer hours) | **Tip** Just across University Avenue from the museum and stretching 138 feet over Ithaca's Fall Creek, the pedestrian bridge was built by Bethlehem Steel Company, builders of the Golden Gate and George Washington Bridges (University Avenue, Ithaca, NY 14850, www.events.cornell.edu).

54 Largest Pancake Griddle

Pass the buckets of maple syrup

Its name contrived from the first letters of "Pennsylvania" and "Yankee," in 1797, Penn Yan's water-powered, community gristmill was acquired by an Englishman named Clarence Birkett who created a private merchant mill, purchasing grain from many growers and selling the flour in neighboring villages in the region. After Birkett's buckwheat flour took first prize at the Paris Exposition of 1887, his products were sought after by grocers across the country. Today, Birkett Mills is one of the largest producers of buckwheat products in the world – buckwheat pancake mixes, cream of buckwheat, and roasted buckwheat (kasha).

In 1996, Birkett Mills held a first-of-its-kind event called the Buckwheat Festival, with events that included making an underwhelming 10-foot-diameter buckwheat pancake. The following year would be more ambitious, and organizers announced they intended to set a world record. They constructed a 28-foot diameter, 10-ton metal pan to cook the largest pancake the world had ever seen.

On Sunday, September 27, 1987, the giant griddle was placed over a bed of hot stones, while batter ingredients were added one by one into the rotating drum of a cement mixer. After 15 gallons of cooking oil was spread on the griddle, the batter was poured down the chute and spread onto the griddle with rakes as it started cooking. The pancake was lifted into the air and flipped by a 75-ton crane, then topped with a 68-pound pat of butter and 15 gallons of maple syrup. The culinary behemoth was cut into 7,200 portions, and attendees each paid one dollar for a taste of history.

The Guinness Book of World Records certified the making of the World's Largest Pancake (exceeded seven years later in Manchester, England). The iconic griddle is now a popular roadside attraction, displayed outside the Birkett Mills complex, an absolute must for shutterbugs.

Address 1 East Main Street, Penn Yan, NY 14527, +1 (315) 536-3311, www.thebirkettmills.com | Getting there Follow Route 54 N or Route 54A N to East Main Street in Penn Yan | Hours Mon–Fri 8am–noon & 1–4:30pm | Tip After selfies at Birkett Mills, walk a block down Main Street to the Wagner Restaurant, the perfect stop for a heaping plate of, you guessed it, buckwheat pancakes (124 East Elm Street, Penn Yan, NY 14527, www.facebook.com/thewagnerrestaurant).

55 The "Lolita" House

Birthplace of Nabokov's nymphet

Vladimir Nabokov's novel *Lolita* has been called both "the filthiest book ever written" and "the best book ever written." The story came to life in Ithaca.

Nabokov arrived at Cornell on July 1, 1948 to teach Russian literature. Following a habit of refusing to set an anchor, never buying a home, he and his wife Vera moved into 957 East State Street, the home of R. B. MacLeod, professor of psychology. Nabokov often wrote in the study, meticulously organizing the novel's complex structure.

It was here in December of 1953 that he finished *Lolita*, the controversial story of a middle-aged professor's obsession with a sexually precocious 12-year-old girl. For many today, a visit to see where he created his masterpiece is akin to a pilgrimage, offering a form of ritualistic homage to the literary genius. While nothing about this private residence hints at its past resident, Nabokov's presence is still very real in Ithaca knowing that the author wrote the seminal novel from a local address.

While the author vehemently denied that his central character was based on any specific individual from his own life, elements of the character were likely influenced by his personal experiences and observations. The MacLeod home had a large photograph hanging over the fireplace mantel picturing 12-year-old daughter Alison. Might Nabokov have imagined her as the nymphet? According to his biographer Brian Boyd, to get details of his central character right, "he would do things like travel on the buses around Ithaca and record phrases, in a little notebook, from young girls that he heard coming back from school."

Within a year after the debut of *Lolita* in 1958, Nabokov left Ithaca. He had earned enough money from the book that he could afford to stop teaching and write full time, and he spent the rest of his life in Montreux, Switzerland. *Lolita* has sold over 50 million copies.

Address 957 East State Street, Ithaca, NY 14850 | **Getting there** From downtown Ithaca, follow East State Street/East Martin Luther King Jr. Street (Route 79) just past the intersection of Valley Road | **Hours** Private home, viewable from the outside only | **Tip** Nabokov's office was in Room 278 of Goldwin Smith Hall on the university Arts Quad. He taught in 250-seat Lecture Room D (among his students was Ruth Bader Ginsburg). If you visit, you'll see a plaque at the second-floor lounge: "In honor of Vladimir Nabokov" (232 Feeney Way, Cornell University, Ithaca, NY 14853).

56 Ludovico Sculpture Trail

Art without borders

It's proof that art doesn't have to be admired exclusively inside a museum. Here, along a one-time canal towpath, and later a bed for the Lehigh Valley Railroad, art and nature come together in perfect harmony, as visitors marvel at sculptures with an outdoor setting as their canvas. Bordering the south bank of the Cayuga-Seneca Canal from Bridge Street to Sucker Brook, these works by contemporary artists, celebrating the history, industry, and people of Seneca Falls, are surrounded by greenery, begging to be explored.

Since the first sculpture, *The Status of Women* by Betty Boggs, was installed in 1999, the walking trail, named for local philanthropist Frank J. Ludovico, has become part of the town's cultural landscape. Among many other works in a variety of artistic styles, Reno Pisano's sculpted plaque depicts the head of Mary Baker Eddy, founder of Christian Science, and a towering metal abstract figure called *Bacchus*, created by Hyon Telarico, represents the mythological god of wine, a connection to the region's wine industry.

Not-to-be-missed is the bronze-cast statue of Amelia Bloomer, the social activist who was known for flouting the custom of women's fashion by wearing loose pantaloons ("bloomers") under her skirts. The work of Geneva-based artist Cherry Rahn depicts Bloomer in a large-brimmed hat, facing outward, making her more approachable to those walking the trail.

Both Women's Rights and Goulds Pumps have deep and meaningful histories in Seneca Falls, and among the trail's most interesting pieces, Audrey Iwanicki's *Working Man's Alchemy*, crafted with actual pump parts – casings, impellers, discharge heads, and motor adapters – is a tribute to the town's major employer since 1848.

The out-and-back trail takes an average of about 30 minutes to complete, from dusk to dawn in all seasons, but best during the fall when changing leaves create their own work of art.

Address 20 Bridge Street, Seneca Falls, NY 13148, www.cnyhiking.com/LudovicoTrail.htm | Getting there From the center of town, cross the Bridge Street Bridge just north of West Bayard Street | Hours Unrestricted | Tip Pulteney Park, in Geneva's historic district, is the site of another outdoor work of art, the *Our Lady of Peace* statue, often clothed in a Santa hat and red cape during the Christmas season, and a Hawaiian skirt and lei in the summer (11 Park Place, Geneva, NY 14456).

57 Mark Twain's Study

Where Tom Sawyer came to life

A licensed riverboat pilot, Samuel Langhorne Clemens spent four years steaming up and down the Mississippi River. Later, as a writer of short stories, he adopted the pen name "Mark Twain," a navigational term for water depth. In 1869, the young man from Hannibal, Missouri was introduced to Olivia "Livy" Langdon, the daughter of a timber and coal magnate from Elmira, who was the richest man in town. A year later, Sam and Livy were married in the Langdon family parlor. The couple settled in Hartford, Connecticut, but Sam would do most of his writing during the 20 summers he spent at Quarry Farm, the Langdon family estate in Elmira.

Throughout most of his life, Sam remained true to two passions, writing and smoking. "I smoke in moderation," he insisted, "only one cigar at a time." Cigars accompanied him from breakfast to bedtime – he indulged in as many as 22 a day – a constant irritation to Livy. Tired of the pervasive smoke invading every room, in 1874, the family arranged to build Sam an isolated study, a good hundred yards uphill from the main house. The study, 12 feet across, with 8 sides and large windows, overlooking Chemung River Valley, was designed to mimic the pilot house of a riverboat, reminiscent of Sam's earlier life. It became his sanctuary, with a desk, bookshelves, and a fireplace for chilly days, where he could write and puff cigars to his heart's content.

In his letters, Sam called the farm "the quietest of all quiet places." It was here, as Mark Twain, that he wrote some of the most beloved works in American literature, where Tom Sawyer, Aunt Polly, Huck Finn, Jim, Injun Joe, and Pudd'nhead Wilson came to life.

In 1952, the historic study was moved from Quarry Farm to the campus of Elmira College, joining bronze statues of the legendary storyteller and his wife Livy. Nearby Cowles Hall contains a Mark Twain exhibit.

Address 800 Park Place (near the corner of Washington and College Avenues), Elmira, NY 14901, +1 (607) 735-1941, www.marktwainstudies.com | Getting there From NY 17, take the Elmira exit, follow signs to the Elmira College campus | Hours Memorial Day–Labor Day Mon–Fri 10am–4:30pm, and by appointment in the off-season | Tip Mark Twain's final resting place is Woodlawn Cemetery. Enter at the gates on the north end of Walnut Street and follow signs to the gravesite. A memorial obelisk in the family plot bears the writer's image (1200 Walnut Street, Elmira, NY 14901, www.cem.va.gov).

58 Memorial Day Museum

The most patriotic town in America

It was a long time coming, but on May 26, 1966, President Lyndon B. Johnson signed a proclamation designating the village of Waterloo as the birthplace of Memorial Day. A federal holiday, held the last Monday in May, is the nation's annual day to honor its deceased servicemen and women.

On April 9, 1865, Robert E. Lee, the Confederate commander, surrendered his army to Union General Ulysses S. Grant at Appomattox, effectively ending the bloodshed of the Civil War. But in the war's aftermath, over 350,000 Union deaths and over 250,000 Confederate deaths were still fresh on the nation's collective mind. That summer, Henry Welles, a Waterloo pharmacist, was the first to suggest that a day be set aside to honor those who had made the ultimate sacrifice. The following year, General John Murray, a local Civil War hero, called on former soldiers to conduct ceremonies and decorate graves of their fallen comrades. But it would be General John Logan, founder of a veterans group called the Grand Army of the Republic, whose political influence helped to establish a national day of remembrance for the Civil War dead. His order served as the basis for a holiday originally called Decoration Day, formalized in Waterloo in 1868.

In 1966, the William H. Burton House, an 1830s Federal-style residence, was purchased by the Waterloo Library and Historical Society to house the solemn museum. A docent greets visitors for a tour that begins at the reproduction of a mourning parlor. The most prominent exhibits relate to the village's role in the history of the holiday, vintage photographs of the main characters in the story, LBJ's pen, and highlight the 1966 Centennial that led to the recognition of Waterloo as the birthplace of Memorial Day.

Waterloo, by the way, holds a spot in *The Guinness Book of World Records* for displaying the most American flags in a single town in one day.

Address 35 East Main Street (Routes 5 & 20), Waterloo, NY 13165, +1 (315) 539-9611, www.waterloony.com | Getting there Follow Routes 5 & 20 into the village of Waterloo, near the intersection of Church Street | Hours May–Sep Thu–Sat noon–5pm | Tip A Civil War cenotaph has stood in the center of Avon's Village Circle since 1877, memorializing the sacrifice made by Avon soldiers. Four cannons are set around the corners of the 45-foot statue (Corner of Genesee Street and Main Street, Avon, NY 14414).

59 Miles Wine Cellars

Visit a haunted winery if you dare!

No winery property in the Finger Lakes has a more fascinating past. Originally a land-grant from the king of England to the Rapalee family, its dock on Seneca Lake once provided area farmers with access to the barges that moved their produce to the cities. An imposing Greek Revival mansion, built in 1802, it became a stop on the Underground Railroad, a shelter for runaway slaves as they made their way north and into Canada, where they could live as free citizens.

In 1978, the Miles family of grape growers purchased the old Rapalee estate to establish Miles Wine Cellars, intent on developing a vineyard on what promised to be a nearly perfect site. Included in the sale were 115 acres of land, the 20-room house, and the Rapalee family cemetery. If you were looking for ghosts, you would probably start your search in a cemetery or in an old, dilapidated house – and this place had both.

One story has it that in 1850, a newlywed couple was hired to work at the home. While in the attic, the man fell to his death, and soon after, his widow died from a broken heart. It wasn't long before folks started reporting strange happenings, and over the years, some have witnessed supernatural activity here. The Miles family, who has had its share of encounters, hired a clairvoyant to confirm that a pair of spirits have been wandering the grounds, causing minor troubles around the house, slamming doors, moving objects, and – boo! – waking the family in the middle of the night. The ghostly couple has at times been seen embracing on the porch, and one of the two might appear on its own as a moving mist.

Miles Wine Cellars has become a hot spot for ghost adventurers and paranormal groupies. To acknowledge the otherworldly residents who haunt the property, the winemaker created a wine appropriately named "Ghost," featuring a shadowy silhouette on the bottle.

Address 168 Randall Crossing Road, Himrod, NY 14842, +1 (607) 243-7742, www.mileswinecellars.com | Getting there Follow Route 14 North from Watkins Glen for 18 miles; make a right turn onto Randall Crossing Road and follow to the winery | Hours Daily 10am–5pm | Tip The "Lady in Granite" is the mysterious appearance of a reclining head on the Gillette family gravestone in Lakeview Cemetery in Penn Yan, believed to be that of Matilda Gillette. Some believe that over time, her whole image will be formed and she will be released to haunt the local community (426 Court Street, Penn Yan, NY 14527).

60 Monet Garden at Mirbeau

A bit of Giverny in Skaneateles

Impressionist artist Claude Monet moved to Giverny, a village 40 miles outside of Paris, in 1883, and began renovating a garden outside his home, inspired by tranquil scenes from his collection of Japanese prints. He diverted a spring to form a pond, planted flowers and willows on the shore, filled the pond with water lilies, then crossed it with a wooden footbridge. The garden was not only a refuge, but also an endless source of inspiration, profoundly influencing the themes of his later works, boldly balancing representation and abstraction.

Aside from the distinctly French-inspired architecture at this Skaneateles inn and spa, the château's buildings surround a garden that evokes the ambiance and artistic spirit of Monet's garden at Giverny. Established in 2000 by Linda and Gary Dower, Mirbeau's interpretation incorporates many of the features that make the original so enchanting – vibrant, densely planted flower beds, a Japanese arched bridge with wisteria vines winding their way along the railings, and four serene, environmentally engineered ponds filled with water lilies and lotus flowers floating on the surface, with koi carp swimming gracefully below.

Beginning in 2014, the garden was revitalized, meticulously landscaped and faithfully refined to honor the artist's vision. The current layout more closely echoes the layered color schemes and organic flow that Monet emphasized, an impressionistic motif with a balance of annuals and perennials, and winding brick paths with vining nasturtiums along the edges, and secluded benches. Surprisingly, Mirbeau welcomes the public to fully immerse in this extraordinary sanctuary.

After the years Monet spent in Giverny, his beloved garden became a place of artistic pilgrimage, just as the garden at Mirbeau has become a modern-day destination for artists, tourists, and gardeners who come to view the living canvas.

Address 851 West Genesee Street (Route 20), Skaneateles, NY 13152, +1 (877) 647-2328, www.mirbeau.com | Getting there From Auburn, follow Route 20 east; from Syracuse, follow Route 20 west | Hours Daily 11am–3pm | Tip It's a short drive into the charming village of Skaneateles to visit Clift Park for a view of the lake Secretary of State William Seward called "the most beautiful body of water in the world" (15 West Genesee Street, Skaneateles, NY 13152, www.townofskaneateles.com).

61 Montezuma Wildlife Refuge

Stopover for frequent flyers

Before settlers arrived in the Finger Lakes region, there was a vast wetland north of Cayuga Lake that extended nearly to Lake Ontario, the remnant of a lake formed when the glaciers retreated back into Canada. The name "Montezuma" was first used in 1806 by Dr. Peter Clark for his hilltop home overlooking the marshes, inspired by his trip to Mexico City and the site of the Aztec chieftain's palace. It would become the name for one of the region's ecological treasures.

The Montezuma National Wildlife Refuge is a crucial stopover for migratory birds traveling the Atlantic Flyway, a major migratory route from Canada to South America. The Flyway hosts an array of bird species, including a wide variety of waterfowl (ducks, geese, and swans), shorebirds, songbirds, and birds of prey like hawks and bald eagles. These birds, attracted by the mixture of nutrient-rich waters, lush and diverse vegetation, and rich invertebrate and insect life, treat the 9,000-acre protected habitat at Montezuma as a kind of B&B, a place to rest, refuel, and breed during their long journeys.

A birdwatching adventure here begins at the visitors center, where one entire wall displays mounted birds you're most likely to see throughout the refuge. There's a stunning replica of an eagle's nest and a "touch table" filled with artifacts collected in the wild. Knowledgeable docents are on hand to answer questions and provide detailed insights into Montezuma's history and ongoing programs. And you can borrow a pair of binoculars here before heading out on a walking trail or taking the Wildlife Drive.

The Seneca Trail follows a one-mile loop, passing a Monarch butterfly waystation, an observation tower, and the Cayuga-Seneca Barge Canal. The Wildlife Drive winds through marshes and wooded areas, providing a front-row seat to the diverse ecosystems.

Address 3395 Route 20, Seneca Falls, NY 13148, +1 (315) 568-5987, www.fws.gov/refuge/montezuma | Getting there From downtown Seneca Falls, follow Route 5 & 20 east for 4 miles | Hours Unrestricted (visitors center Apr–Nov 10am–3pm, weather depending) | Tip At Sapsucker Woods in Ithaca, birdwatchers hike along 4 miles of trails, weaving through deep woods, atop boardwalks in swamps, and beside ponds bursting with feathered wildlife of all kinds, in the 230-acre sanctuary (159 Sapsucker Woods Road, Ithaca, NY 14850, www.birds.cornell.edu).

62 Motor Racing Center

No speed limit here

Watkins Glen will forever have a place in racing history. It was here, on October 2, 1948, that the first road race was held after World War II. The six-and-a-half-mile circuit ran through the village streets, starting and ending in front of the local courthouse. For 20 years, the world's best drivers and fastest cars descended on this small Finger Lakes village, and three times beat Monte Carlo and other glamorous Formula One venues to be named the best-organized Grand Prix event of the season. *Sports Illustrated* described the charm of the Watkins Glen Grand Prix as "courage and cornpone, sophistication with straw in its teeth."

So it's only natural that the Glen would become home to the International Motor Racing Research Center. Think of it as a museum inside a library. Opened in June 1999 and sharing a building with the public library, the IMRRC has more than 700 individual collections, representing the heritage of amateur and professional motor racing. You'll find more than 3,800 rare and reference books, over 2,800 cataloged race programs, 4,500 cataloged films, nearly 800 periodical titles, and photographs in the tens of thousands.

Archives include the personal papers of drivers, journalists, and authors, as well as the records and newsletters of clubs and motor racing teams, historical photographs, films, oral histories, and memorabilia. The amount of information available here can seem overwhelming but it's well organized and easy to access.

The center welcomes both serious researchers and casual fans, and the first thing you'll see is one of the race cars on loan – it could be anything from an IndyCar to a dragster, a different car nearly every month. Knowledgeable research and archives staff members are on hand to share their passion with all who visit, and you'll be invited to watch a 25-minute video on racing history in Watkins Glen.

Address 610 South Decatur Street, Watkins Glen, NY 14891, +1 (607) 535-9044, www.racingarchives.org | Getting there From South Franklin Street in downtown Watkins Glen, take Grandview Avenue to South Decatur Street | Hours Mon–Fri 9am–5pm, some Sat 10am–4pm during race weekends (check website for details) | Tip A local tour of the Drivers Walk of Fame is a walk through racing history, honoring drivers who competed in those early street races, from 1948 to 1952. The majority of markers are located along the east and west sidewalks of Franklin Street in downtown Watkins Glen.

63 Museum of the Earth

Visitors from the Jurassic age

It all began with a dispute over the safety of his fossil collection. Gilbert D. Harris, a Cornell University professor from 1894 to 1934, was nearing retirement and intended to leave thousands of priceless fossils and research papers to the university, on condition that the geology department would provide a secure fireproof building with non-flammable furnishings. When Cornell failed to comply, Harris packed up the collection and took it home – literally. He built his own facility of concrete, with metal fixtures, next to his home in Ithaca's Cayuga Heights neighborhood. It was the start of the Paleontological Research Institution, chartered as an independent educational institution by the state of New York in 1933.

In 2003, PRI opened to the public as the Museum of the Earth, an 18,000-square-foot facility overlooking Cayuga Lake, housing one of the largest collections of invertebrate fossils in North America, and now formally affiliated with Cornell.

The museum spans the various ages of Earth's history with permanent exhibits, including a 500-foot-long series of tiles with images of fossils in intervals of time over the past 544 million years. Among the most dramatic exhibits are the 44-foot skeleton of a North Atlantic right whale in the lobby, and one of the most complete and well-preserved skeletons of a North American mastodon, an extinct relative of modern elephants, found buried beneath a backyard pond in Hyde Park, New York.

Everyone's favorite is "Steggy," a Stegosaurus sculpture made in 1904 for the Smithsonian Institution's Museum of Natural History. The papier-mâché model represents what most experts at the time believed this dinosaur looked like when he was alive. After Steggy made his first public appearance at the St. Louis World's Fair, he was returned to the Smithsonian for display until officially donated to the Museum of the Earth in 2015.

Address 1259 Trumansburg Road, Ithaca, NY 14850, +1 (607) 273-6623, www.museumoftheearth.org | Getting there From downtown Ithaca, follow Trumansburg Road (Route 96) for one mile | Hours Thu–Mon 10am–5pm | Tip Fossil hunters can get to see (but not touch) thousands of individual fossil horn corals at Staghorn Cliffs above Skaneateles Lake, one of New York's premiere paleontological sites, reachable by boat or kayak from Andrew R. Fuller Park (7330 Glen Haven Road, Homer, NY 13077, www.scott-ny.org).

64 Myers Point Lighthouse

Keeping watch over Cayuga Lake

The Point takes its name from Andrew Myers, who settled here with his family in 1792 and began building flat-bottom boats to carry freight from the lake and through the early canals to big city markets. It's also the site of Cayuga Lake's first salt well, drilled to reach the salt deposits left from the shallow sea that once covered the region. The Cayuga Salt Company evaporated the brine for fine table salt and other salt products until 1959, when, as salt production on the Point wound down, the company donated 24 acres of land to the town for a lakeside park.

Most of the donated land was marsh and ponds, so the Town of Lansing Highway Department went to work, draining the area and grading the land to create a stable foundation for park features. Today, Myers Park is a vibrant public space that spans 31 acres of lawns, including graceful old trees, shrubs, and flowers along the shore, with panoramic views up and down the lake. It has a swimming area, picnic areas and pavilions, playground, volleyball net, basketball courts, horseshoe pits, a marina and boat launches, canoe and kayak rentals, and a designated camping area.

In 1998, local residents proposed an ambitious plan to build a lighthouse on the shore of their park. Constructed from 3,000 individually cut and donated bricks, the 25-foot-tall lighthouse, though not a traditional navigational beacon, was created as a community project by local volunteers. Now a popular backdrop for weddings, festivals, and photo opportunities, it keeps watch over the lake with a single strobe light that flashes every six seconds from dawn to dusk, April to November every year, visible from 10 miles away.

Across Salmon Creek from the park, the Salt Point Preserve is a scenic peninsula with walking trails, native trees and shrubs, and vital wildlife. Over 230 bird species have been recorded in the Salt Point vicinity.

Address 1 Lansing Park Road, Lansing, NY 14882, +1 (607) 533-7388, www.lansingrec.com | **Getting there** Follow Route 34B (Ridge Road) in Lansing to Myers Road, then to Lansing Park Road | **Hours** Daily 7am until dark | **Tip** After the Central Exchange Hotel became a gathering place for horse thieves, folks started calling it Rogues Harbor, and the name stuck. One mile from Myers Point, today's Rogues Harbor is a tavern and inn (2079 East Shore Drive, Lansing, NY 14882, www.rogueshaarbor.com).

65_Namgyal Monastery

Well, hello Dalai

Your path to enlightenment begins here. Since 1959, natives of Tibet have scattered throughout the world, fleeing the Communist Chinese occupation of their country. Among the first Tibetan refugees to arrive in Ithaca in 1992 was a monk from Namgyal, the Dalai Lama's monastery in Dharamshala, India. With his inspiration and the help of American friends, a Victorian house on Aurora Street was transformed into a cultural and religious center for the Tibetan community, growing to become the North American Seat of His Holiness the 14th Dalai Lama, his personal monastery, blessed during his visit to Ithaca in 2007.

You might ask why the Dalai Lama selected a small town like Ithaca from dozens of cities to be the site of an international center for Buddhism. Ithaca is a "sanctuary city," among the first Tibetan resettlement communities in the United States, and Namgyal serves as a cultural center for the Tibetan refugee community living here.

In 2014, Namgyal moved up to South Hill, establishing a new temple complex, including the Dalai Lama's library and a small museum. For its primary mission, the Namgyal Monastery offers Western students the opportunity to study authentic Tibetan Buddhism in a monastic setting. It acts as a hub in the academic world, connecting scholars and institutions throughout North America and the world. The monks teach classes on philosophy, Buddhism, Tibetan language, and meditation to visitors or students of any faith. Guided meditations are offered on Mondays, Wednesdays, and Fridays, open to anyone in the community.

It was the Buddhist monks here who guided Kurt Cobain, member of the grunge band Nirvana, along the path to his next life. In July 1994, three months after Cobain's passing, his widow, Courtney Love, brought his ashes to Namgyal, where they were consecrated by the monks, mixed with clay, and molded to make sculptural tsatsas.

Address 201 Tibet Drive, Ithaca, NY 14850, +1 (607) 272-2785, www.namgyal.org | **Getting there** Beginning in downtown Ithaca, follow Route 96B (Danby Road) south for 3 miles to Tibet Drive (on left) | **Hours** Mon–Fri 9am–6pm | **Tip** On display at Namgyal, the Dalai Lama's 1966 Land Rover, with license plate HIM 755, was the official vehicle of His Holiness the Dalai Lama for 10 years, from 1966 to 1976. The vehicle was mostly driven by Cheogyal, who ferried him along the mountainous roads of Dharamshala, India.

66 Naples 9/11 Memorial

A community's solemn space

After the tragic events of September 11, 2001, thousands of artifacts from the World Trade Center were salvaged from the debris and stored at JFK Airport's Hangar 17, preserved with the intention of sharing them with communities across the country and around the world. The Port Authority of New York and New Jersey, owners of the World Trade Center, established a program to donate these relics, focusing on community requests for memorial projects. The initiative allowed cities, fire departments, police stations, schools, and other organizations to receive pieces of the towers at no cost.

After Fire Chief Patrick Elwell of the Maxfield Hose Company submitted a preliminary design for a village memorial in Naples, the Port Authority approved a chunk of scorched steel, and beginning with delivery of the piece, the local community rallied behind volunteer firefighters, contributing resources and support, donating materials and funds, all in an effort to participate in the larger national remembrance.

That 10-foot section of a steel I-beam from the towers, a sobering relic of the tragedy, serves as the memorial's centerpiece. The Ground Zero artifact is surrounded by a semi-circular stone enclosure with two granite pillars, representing the Twin Towers, each inscribed with details on time of impact, time of collapse, civilian lives lost, NYFD and other first responder lives lost, as well as lives lost on American Airlines Flight 11. Placement of the pillars is true to the geographic position of the North and South towers in New York. Three flags fly overhead, the American flag, the state flag, and the fire department "Loyal to Our Duty" flag.

On the five-year anniversary of 9/11, the village unveiled the memorial, a commemorative setting facing Main Street, a visible and accessible location that invites both locals and visitors to pause and pay their respects.

Address 148 South Main Street (corner of Vine Street), Naples, NY 14512, www.naplesny.us | Getting there Route 21 (along the west side of Canandaigua Lake) becomes Main Street in Naples | Hours Unrestricted | Tip John Jacob Widmer established a winery here over 150 years ago, and Naples' identity is indelibly connected to grape growing. The village embraces grape culture with purple fire hydrants, grape pies, and the annual Naples Grape Festival.

67 Newfield Covered Bridge

Drive through an endangered species

Franklin Pierce was President and potato chips were invented. The year was 1853, and the good citizens of Newfield agreed to construct a bridge across the West Branch of Cayuga Creek, connecting the village road to Ithaca, a few miles to the north.

After stonemasons laid abutments, carpenters used local timbers to construct the lattice truss bridge, an uninterrupted series of crisscross diagonals, 115 feet long and 16 feet wide. The men worked from sunrise to sunset for a dollar a day, and locally milled lumber was purchased for six dollars per 1,000 board feet. The total cost of the bridge was $800.

Like many other rural bridges at the time, the Newfield bridge was enclosed with sides and a peaked roof to shield structural components from the harsh effects of upstate weather and extend its lifespan. At first, solid siding ran the length of the bridge, but diamond-shaped openings were later cut to admit light.

Although the bridge survived a historic flood in 1905, supporting timbers degraded and deteriorated over time. In 1969, the county highway department deemed the structure unsafe, and the beloved bridge was in danger of being torn down. Luckily, the New York State Covered Bridge Society was successful in convincing the highway department of the historical importance of the bridge, and restoration efforts were begun.

Rotting wood was replaced, interior arch supports were added, and the roof was raised two feet to allow for a 26-foot clearance. The old siding was replaced with hemlock planks, the roof's shingles replaced with white cedar. The entire structure was raised one foot and repainted in its historic red.

Newfield Covered Bridge is the last survivor of the three covered bridges erected in the Finger Lakes region. It remains the oldest covered bridge in New York State that still allows motor vehicle traffic.

Address 20 Bridge Street, Newfield, NY 14867 | **Getting there** Follow State Route 13 eight miles south of Ithaca, take exit at the circle to Newfield, and follow Main Street to the bridge | **Hours** Unrestricted | **Tip** On October 24, 1910, former president Theodore Roosevelt arrived in Newfield to the cheers of 250 townspeople. He delivered a rousing speech from the balcony of the Newfield Hotel, now an apartment building (182 Main Street, Newfield, NY 14857).

68 Newtown Battlefield

A victory for the Continental Army

John Sullivan emerged as a pivotal figure in young America's struggle for independence. The son of Irish settlers from County Cork, Ireland, he was promoted to Major General on August 9, 1776. He commanded troops during the Battle of Princeton, where his leadership caught the attention of George Washington.

In the summer of 1779, General Washington ordered Sullivan to drive Iroquois tribes from their settlements as punishment for siding with the British and launching attacks against Patriot communities. Sullivan's force began a march along the Chemung River Valley when they encountered their first major resistance near the village of Newtown. On August 29, the British relied on their Indigenous allies to halt the colonists, but outnumbered at least five to one, they proved incapable of withstanding the onslaught. Sullivan operated virtually unopposed for the next month, allowing him to proceed further north, burning every structure, obliterating orchards, and fulfilling Washington's directive to completely destroy the native settlements.

While the 2,000-acre battlefield was declared a National Historic Landmark in 1965, a 372-acre portion of the battlefield is now protected and managed as a state park. Its main attraction is a 1,400-foot wooded area called Sullivan Hill, once fortified by the Iroquois in a bid to ambush Sullivan's troops.

A monument was dedicated at the top of the hill on August 29, 1879, the centennial of the battle. The present 80-foot granite obelisk was erected in 1912, and during the 1930s, Civilian Conservation Corps crews built and developed many of the present facilities of the park. As you walk back to the dramatic overlook, you'll pass another stone monument, this one placed in the park by the state of New Hampshire, in memory of Sullivan, the hero of Newtown, who went on to become governor of the Granite State.

Address 2346 County Road 60, Elmira, NY 14901, +1 (607) 732-6067, www.parks.ny.gov | Getting there Take the Jerusalem Hill Road exit off Route 86, turn onto Brant Road (Route 60 – becomes Oneida Road), drive 3 miles to the park entrance | Hours Daily 6am–6pm | Tip From Elmira, take Route 13 N to Ithaca, a 30-mile drive. Your ride follows along the trail of the Sullivan Campaign to Tutelo Park, honoring the legacy of the Tutelo tribe who lived peacefully here until 1779 (197 Bostwick Road, Ithaca, NY 14850, www.thehistorycenter.net/ithaca-heritage).

69 Old Cobblestone Church

Built during the region's "stone age"

In 1825, stonemasons who had worked on the Erie Canal began constructing cobblestone buildings, developing an eccentric architectural style. Smooth, round stones that took shape after years of being tossed in the tumble of shifting glacial remains were cleared from the fields by early farmers. With a seemingly endless supply of these similarly shaped and sized stones, the idea of using them as building materials quickly gained popularity. The skilled masons constructed homes, municipal buildings, garden walls, and churches, making the Finger Lakes region home to the largest concentration of cobblestone structures in the nation.

The Unitarian Universalist Church, built in 1837 as a Universalist Church and steeped in history and lore, is the oldest building in Cortland County and one of only two such cobblestone buildings in the country. Its vernacular, Quaker-inspired "Meeting House" design, typical of many early meeting houses of the period, reflects the building's past as a central hub for social reformers, activists, and assorted rabble-rousers who frequently visited here.

Speakers traveling the lecture circuit who made stops at the Universalist Church included women's rights advocate Susan B. Anthony; Clara Barton, founder of the American Red Cross; abolitionist Henry Ward Beecher; essayist and poet Ralph Waldo Emerson; Christian pacifist William Lloyd Garrison; and Harriet Beecher Stowe, author of *Uncle Tom's Cabin*.

The "old cobblestone church" was Cortland's first town hall until 1885, and with no requirement for separation of church and state at that time, the church served the dual purpose of being both a place for feisty town meetings and solemn worship. Over the years, citizens of Cortland have used the building to vote, to conduct government, to teach grade school, to hold concerts, and to hear progressive ideas from the lectern.

Address 3 Church Street, Cortland, NY 13045, +1 (607) 753-0020, www.uucortlandny.org | **Getting there** Follow Route 13 (Clinton Avenue) to Church Street | **Hours** Services on Sundays Sep–Jun 10:30am | **Tip** The historic Terra Cotta Building in Alfred was built almost entirely of bricks, ornamental terracotta, and roofing tiles; so unique it served as inspiration for one constructed at the 1893 World's Fair (62 North Main Street, Alfred, NY 14802, www.alleganyhistory.org).

70 Painted Post Monument

How the town got its name

The town's name is rooted in Native American history and local legend. It seems an actual "painted post" once stood at the confluence of the Cohocton, Tioga, and Chemung Rivers, and most have come to believe that it was created to honor Montour, a Seneca chieftain who was killed in battle, marking a place of respect and memory. His comrades buried him by the riverside, and planted the post above his grave, adorned with painted symbols to commemorate the sacred site, each symbol telling a story of his bravery.

The post stood for many years after white settlement, and it had such a profound impression on early settlers that when the county was founded in 1796, they named the village after it. The post weathered away over time, and in the summer of 1893, a campaign was launched to fund the construction of a stone monument topped with a metal silhouette of a Seneca chief. At the turn of the 20th century, a more life-like version was crafted by a local blacksmith. During a storm in November of 1948, a fierce wind toppled the chief from his pedestal, and upon impact, the sculpture shattered into fragments. At a town meeting held on April 7, 1949, citizens of the village approved a proposal to replace the damaged sculpture.

The current monument depicts Chief Montour with his arm raised, measuring eight feet from the base to the tip of his lifted hand, standing at a post that rises to 12 feet. The figures were first modeled in soft clay, supported by a steel armature, then crafted in plaster and cast in bronze. The new supporting stone pedestal was partially funded with pennies donated by the schoolchildren of Painted Post, and a plaque was installed on the base, summarizing the story of the village's namesake.

Dedication of the monument took place on May 30, 1950, as 15,000 people crowded on newly named Chief Montour Square to witness the unveiling.

Address Intersection of North Hamilton Street and West Water Street, Painted Post, NY 14870, www.villageofpaintedpost.com | Getting there Exit Route 86 (Southern Tier Expressway) at Painted Post, follow North Hamilton Street to West Water Street | Hours Unrestricted | Tip Chief Montour was the son of "Queen" Catharine Montour, wife of Seneca chief Telenemut, who assumed leadership of a village that would become known as Catherine's Town, after her husband was killed. The story is told on a historical marker at the intersection of Route 14 and Havana Glen Road in Montour Falls.

71 Peter Whitmer Farm

Cradle of Mormonism

In the early 1880s, the Finger Lakes region was so ablaze with spiritual fervor, it was called "the burned-over district." In rural Fayette, the 100-acre Peter Whitmer Farm became the site of a powerful religious movement that would go on to change the spiritual landscape forever. It was here on April 6, 1830, that a charismatic young man named Joseph Smith and his followers formally established the Church of Jesus Christ of Latter-day Saints.

The faithful believe that Smith unearthed a set of gold plates or tablets at the direction of an angel named Moroni, who commanded him to translate the ancient text into what is now known as the Book of Mormon. Smith spent six months at the Whitmer log home, where a large part of the translation took place, and where he received revelations from God to start a new church.

The Peter Whitmer Farm is now a historic site, owned and operated by the Church of Jesus Christ of Latter-day Saints since 1926. The visitors' center includes artifacts, paintings, and interactive displays on the formation, early growth, and continuing legacy of the church. Visitors are welcomed by church missionaries and invited on a tour, beginning with a 23-minute film that depicts Joseph Smith completing the translation of the Book of Mormon and the organization of the church.

A tour includes a visit to the nearby replica of the original Whitmer log home. Reconstructed by historical architects in 1980 to mark the sesquicentennial of the church's founding, the interior's 19th-century recreation features a living area, main-floor bedroom, and upstairs bedrooms. The west upstairs bedroom is significant – it includes a table with a lantern, where Joseph Smith wrote the Book of Mormon. A visit here is a rewarding experience for people of all faiths, and a fascinating insight into history, culture, and the pioneering spirit that shaped a community.

Address 1451 Aunkst Road, Waterloo, NY 13165, +1 (315) 539-2552, www.churchofjesuschrist.org | Getting there From Seneca Falls, follow Route 96 south to Aunkst Road | Hours Mon–Sat 10am–7pm, Sun 1–7pm | Tip The Hill Cumorah Visitors' Center in Palmyra (40 minutes away) commemorates the place where Joseph Smith found the "golden plates." A self-guided tour tells the story of the Mormon Church (603 State Route 21, Palmyra, NY 14522).

72 Ports of New York

Winery as a work of art

Finger Lakes winemaking has perhaps found its most unlikely location – the "other side of the tracks" in Ithaca's industrial West End. This is not only the region's most eccentric winery, but a venture conceived as a work of art unto itself. The artist and winemaker, Frédéric Robert Bouché, comes from a long line of vintners in his native France. His great-great-grandfather owned vineyards in Bordeaux. His great-grandfather made wines at Maison Bouché in the Calvados appellation of Normandy. And, growing up, Frédéric worked with his grandfather, training in family techniques he now uses to craft fortified wines that mimic wines from Portugal's Douro region.

After studies at the École Supérieure des Arts Modernes in Paris, Frédéric became an installation artist, creating immersive, often large-scale, pieces. The urban winery, with its painstaking attention to detail, is perhaps his most impressive installation, while his artistic background has influenced a creative and interdisciplinary approach to winemaking.

Although his winery is named Ports of New York, according to international agreements, the wines cannot be called "Ports" since they're not produced in Portugal. Unlike producers who imitate Port wines with lesser quality varietals, Frédéric contracts for premium local grapes and fortifies the wines with distilled spirits of native Catawba. The wines are made using a traditional solera system, blending from a series of French oak barrels holding wines that have been aged from 4 to 17 years. While inspired by the venerable Portuguese originals, his wines are truly singular products of the region.

Red Meleau is based on Cabernet Franc and White Meleau is made with Muscat Ottonel. The red version is most appropriately served at room temperature for consumption after a meal. Follow the French habit of chilling and serving the white version as an aperitif.

Address 815 Taber Street, Ithaca, NY 14850, +1 (607) 220-6317, www.portsofnewyork.com | **Getting there** Follow West State Street to Ithaca's West End neighborhood, turn left onto Taber Street and the winery is just around the corner | **Hours** Fri–Mon noon–6pm – wine tastings and self-guided tours available | **Tip** Drive into downtown to visit the sculpture of Frances Perkins, who served in President Franklin Roosevelt's administration from 1933 to 1945. As Secretary of Labor, she was the architect of the New Deal and Social Security. Perkins taught at Cornell from 1957 to 1965 (100 West Seneca Street, Ithaca, NY 14850).

73 The "Queen's Castle"

Summer camp of the bluestockings

Founded in the summer of 1875 by Elizabeth Smith Miller, her daughter, and five friends, all of whom were active in the suffrage movement and social reform causes, Fossenvue, its name an anagram for "seven of us," served as a retreat where an eclectic and progressive group could engage in activities unrestricted by society's norms. Here, halfway down Seneca Lake from the Miller estate in Geneva, they played tennis, practiced archery, hiked trails, and as liberated women, shed clothing to swim in the lake.

Fossenvue thrived in an atmosphere of lively dialogue and thoughtful debate. For one month each summer, the women gathered to discuss philosophy and societal innovation. Ideas about freedom, equality, and justice were explored in a setting that encouraged thought and open conversation.

During 26 years of camp life, they were joined by prominent suffragists, writers, and thinkers, such as Elizabeth Cady Stanton, author and activist; Susan B. Anthony, feminist social reformer; Felix Adler, founder of the Ethical Culture Society; Alice Stone Blackwell, a radical socialist; Louis Agassiz Fuertes, renowned ornithologist; Anna Comstock, naturalist and educator; and Dr. Emily Blackwell, one of the first female doctors in the United States.

In 1899, the largest permanent structure at Fossenvue was erected as a birthday present for Elizabeth Smith Miller, "the Queen of Fossenvue." The 17-square-foot cabin, with lofty raftered ceiling and high, massive fireplace, dubbed the "Queen's Castle," was built by seven men; begun on the seventh of the month, and finished in seven days. It's the only building that remains to tell the story of the idyllic camp, now part of Finger Lakes National Forest. Follow the trail from the parking area, about a 10-minute hike along steep gravel switchbacks, descending through forest to the site of Fossenvue and the "Queen's Castle."

Address 9698 Route 414, Lodi, NY 14860, +1 (802) 747-6700, www.gofingerlakes.org | Getting there Follow Route 414 to Caywood Point | Hours Unrestricted (Memorial Day–Labor Day), viewable from the outside only | Tip The design of the Shalestone Winery tasting room building, across from the entrance to the campsite, was inspired by the "Queen's Castle" cabin at Fossenvue (9681 Route 414, Lodi, NY 14860, www.shalestonevineyards.com).

74 Rod Serling Grave

Gatekeeper to the Twilight Zone

For countless fans of *The Twilight Zone* scattered across the globe, the Lakeview Cemetery in the sleepy village of Interlaken is considered the "Rod Serling cemetery." In other words, the place that has been his "home" since June 1975.

Rodman Edward Serling was born in Syracuse in 1924 and grew up in Binghamton. He joined the army after graduating from high school, and during World War II, earned a Purple Heart and Bronze Star for his bravery and injuries sustained during the battle for Manila. After being discharged from the army in 1946, he enrolled in Antioch College, where he developed interests in theater, writing, and broadcasting.

Serling worked in radio and television for a number of years before creating *The Twilight Zone*. The anthology series premiered on CBS on October 2, 1959, and besides his roles as head writer and producer, Serling presented each iconic opening narration, holding a cigarette and setting the stage for each intriguing and provocative episode. Produced by Cayuga Productions and named for Cayuga Lake, where he owned a family cottage, the series became a major influence on television and American popular culture. To this day, the series maintains a devoted following, and reruns are still shown regularly on the Syfy channel.

From the late 1960s until his untimely death at age 50, Serling taught courses on film criticism, writing, and drama at Ithaca College. His final resting place at Lakeview Cemetery, not far from his beloved lakeside home, is marked with a simple granite stone, a reminder of his service during World War II. Located in the northeast corner of the burial area (lot 1044), it has become a sort of outdoor sanctuary, where fans visit to pay tribute. Some leave simple signs of their presence or place stones in Jewish tradition, others bring pieces of paper bearing quotes from favorite *Twilight Zone* episodes.

Address 3675 County Road 150, Interlaken, NY 14847, +1 (607) 280-2099, www.lake-viewcemetery.com | Getting there From Route 96, turn onto County Road 150 | Hours Unrestricted | Tip The Rod Serling Archive is preserved at the Bundy Museum in Binghamton (one hour away). You can view rare artifacts, original wire images, TV and film props, memorabilia and personal items (127–129 Main Street, Binghamton, NY 13905, www.bundymuseum.org).

75 Sagan Planet Walk

Passport through the solar system

If you've ever wondered about the sizes of planets in the Solar System or the distances between them, maybe you should take a walk across Ithaca.

As a professor of astronomy and co-founder of the Planetary Society, Dr. Carl Edward Sagan spent most of his career at Cornell University in Ithaca, where he published more than 600 scientific papers and articles and was author, co-author, or editor of more than 20 books. In his best-selling 1980 book *Cosmos*, as well as in the television series of the same name, he discussed the vast distances between planets in the Solar System and beyond. One of his famous analogies involved imagining the Solar System as a scale model where Earth is reduced to the size of a marble, illustrating the scale of the universe in simple terms and emphasizing humanity's place within it.

In 1997, a year after Sagan's passing, the Sagan Planet Walk, an exhibition named in his memory, was installed across downtown Ithaca, stretching along a three-quarter-mile route that takes visitors on a tour of the scaled Solar System, putting the massive distances into human perspective. Each "planet station" along neighborhood sidewalks features a monolithic structure and interpretive plaque with NASA images, and models illustrating the size of each planet as it compares to the Sun.

The course starts at the Sun and works its way outward, passing the closely spaced Mercury, Venus, Earth, and Mars. After Mars, the planets become more distant; the next stop is Jupiter, then Saturn, followed by a long gap to reach Uranus. Crossing the Carl Sagan Bridge over Cascadilla Creek leads to Neptune, and along the way, there's a 4.5-billion-year-old meteorite at a station representing the asteroid belt. The walk goes all the way to Pluto at the Sciencenter, a hands-on science museum, where visitors can explore further exhibits and learn more about space and astronomy.

Address 171 The Commons to 601 1st Street, Ithaca, NY 14850, +1 (607) 272-0600, www.saganplanetwalk.com; Bill Nye, "The Science Guy," narrates a companion audio tour of the Planet Walk by cell phone at +1 (703) 637-6237 | **Getting there** From downtown Ithaca; the walk begins on The Commons, a four-block pedestrian shopping area. Locate the Sun model at the center of The Common | **Hours** Unrestricted | **Tip** While teaching at Cornell, Sagan lived in the former headquarters of the secret Sphinx Head Society, perched on the edge of a cliff overlooking Ithaca's Fall Creek gorge, designed to resemble an Egyptian tomb (900 Stewart Avenue, Ithaca, NY 14850).

76 Schooner *True Love*

Romance on the high seas

It was always a symbol of privilege and upper-class lifestyle. Commissioned in 1926 by millionaire Bostonian Elmer J. Bliss, the sailing vessel *Verona II* was designed and built by John G. Alden in Wiscasset, Maine by Pendleton Brothers Shipyard. Its handsome, 67-foot hull was crafted in Southern pine and finished with mahogany trim. Twin masts rise 58 feet in the sky.

In 1940, the schooner became inspiration for the *True Love* in the 1940 romantic comedy *The Philadelphia Story* with Cary Grant and Katharine Hepburn, where she appeared as a miniature model of herself, and in Hepburn's words, "My, she was yar." Sixteen years later, the lifesize *True Love* was borrowed by the MGM studio for her movie debut in *High Society*, the 1956 musical remake with Bing Crosby, Grace Kelly, Frank Sinatra, and Louis Armstrong.

In the film, the *True Love* is owned by C. K. Dexter-Haven, played by Bing Crosby, and in a memorable flashback aboard the yacht, Crosby sings "True Love" to Grace Kelly, who portrays Tracy Lord, his former wife. The scene was filmed in Newport Beach, Rhode Island, and after her movie career, the schooner took up residency in St. Thomas. In 2008, she sailed up the Hudson River, across the Erie Canal, and down into Seneca Lake harbor.

Today, owner Terry Stewart and captain Bill Holgate sail a fully restored *True Love*, certified by the Coast Guard for up to 22 passengers, up to four times a day, depending on weather and time of the year. Passengers receive a safety briefing, a telling of the schooner's history, and a glass of Finger Lakes sparkling wine before heading out on a two-hour voyage. You won't be surprised to learn that a vessel named *True Love* is one of the region's most romantic attractions – no better place to pop the question, hold wedding parties, celebrate anniversaries, renew vows, or simply share an adventure on Seneca Lake.

Address Harbor Park Pier, 214 North Franklin Street, Watkins Glen, NY 14891, +1 (607) 535-5253, www.sailtruelove.com | **Getting there** Take Route 14 into downtown Watkins Glen (becomes North Franklin Street); the Pier is at the southern point of the lake | **Hours** See website for details of public sailing days and private bookings | **Tip** To complete a romantic getaway, plan a nearby stay at the Idlwilde Inn, an 1890s-era Victorian-mansion-turned-B&B, perched at the top of a hill overlooking Seneca Lake (1 Lakeview Avenue, Watkins Glen, NY 14891, www.idlwildeinn.com).

77 Sciencenter Playground

For the young and young at heart

Established in 1983, the Sciencenter in Ithaca has since grown to become a nationally recognized institution. In a remarkable collaborative effort, 2,000 community volunteers joined forces to construct the iconic 5,000-square-foot museum and adjacent playground. The complex features a diverse array of engaging educational programs, hands-on learning experiences, exhibits including live animals, astronomy, sustainability, and an engaging outdoor space for creative play and discovery.

Over the years, the Sciencenter has undergone a series of renovations and transformations, most notably with the contribution of Bill Nye, "The Science Guy," Cornell grad and visiting professor, who has enhanced the educational offerings.

The multi-level, interactive playground offers hands-on experiences that delve into concepts of sound, motion, water, and physics. Young adventurers create melodies with steel drums and bells, exploring sound and rhythm; bounce on the world's only Kevlar cable suspension bridge, challenging their balance and fine motor coordination; communicate across distances by exploring sound waves with whisper dishes; create bubbles of all shapes and sizes at the bubble station; and "excavate" to uncover hidden treasures at the sand table.

For the youngest explorers, ages four and under, the Curiosity Playground provides a dedicated space for crawling, climbing, and discovery. And, at the Little Sprouts Farmers Market simulation, children plant and harvest toy vegetables, transport them in toy wheelbarrows, and sell their produce at the market using a cash register. Open-ended structures encourage children to create their own narratives and explore freely.

A community hub, the playground provides a dynamic environment where children learn while they play, and the family-friendly designs encourage parents to actively engage in their child's world.

Address 601 1st Street, Ithaca, NY 14850, +1 (607) 272-0600, www.sciencenter.org | **Getting there** From Route 13 north, turn right onto 3rd Street, left onto Franklin Street, then left onto 1st Street | **Hours** Tue–Sun 10am–5pm (Apr–Oct), also Mon during school breaks | **Tip** Ithaca Children's Garden, located within Cass Park, is a garden-based, hands-on learning and free-play experience for children of all ages, home to "Gaia," a larger-than-life turtle sculpture (121 Turtle Lane, Ithaca, NY 14850, www.ithacachildrensgarden.org).

78 Seneca Council Grounds

Native American sacred site

In 1906, industrialist William Pryor Letchworth bequeathed his 1,000-acre estate to New York State, which became the core of Letchworth State Park. The towering rock walls that can soar up to 550 feet have earned the nickname "Grand Canyon of the East." Its deep gorges, scenic trails, and breathtaking waterfalls attract visitors from around the world, not only for the stunning landscapes, but also for the preservation of Native American history. The area holds special significance for the Seneca Nation, who once lived and thrived here.

Marking the place where the tribal council of Seneca elders gathered around council fires, the historic grounds at the park consist of the Council House, Nancy Jemison cabin, Mary Jemison statue, and rustic viewing pavilion.

Mary Jemison was born in 1743, on board the ship that was bringing her family from Northern Ireland to America. During the French and Indian War, Mary and her family were captured by Shawnee warriors, and while her parents and siblings were killed, Mary was spared, and later adopted by the Senecas. Rather than returning to colonial life after her capture, Mary fully embraced her new life within the community. She learned the language, adopted their customs, and formed lasting bonds with her new family. Known as "The White Woman of the Genesee," her story is well documented in literature, inspiration for *The Searchers*, the 1956 film starring John Wayne.

Her seven-foot-high bronze statue, depicting Mary carrying her first child, was erected in 1910 and stands near her final resting place in the Council Grounds. The site includes displays that interpret the history of the Seneca Nation, their customs, governance structure, and their relationship with settlers. To access the grounds, take the Iroquois Clan Trail beginning behind the Letchworth Museum, or drive up Council Grounds Road to the parking area.

Address 1 Letchworth State Park, Castile, NY 14427, +1 (585) 493-3600, www.parks.ny.gov/parks/letchworth | Getting there From Route 39, take Denton Corners Road to the Castile entrance | Hours Daily 6am–11pm | Tip Another park statue, nicknamed "Iron Mike," honors the experience and achievements of the more than 3,000 men who served in CCC camps here during the Great Depression-era (the road to the marker is off the main north-south park road between the visitors center and the Castile entrance).

79__Seneca "Ghost Deer"

Catch me if you can

The Finger Lakes region has a little-known nuclear history, serving as a storage site for weapons linked to the Manhattan Project. While the Department of Defense has never officially confirmed it, the Seneca Army Depot in Romulus likely housed the East Coast's largest stockpile of nuclear weapons during the Cold War. The once-secret complex is now best known as home to an exceedingly rare breed of white-tailed deer.

First discovered by Army personnel after the depot was developed and surrounded by a 24-mile-long fence, the world's largest herd of the mystical white "ghost deer," a species with a genetic anomaly, has been restricted to its boundaries ever since. Limited predators and controlled hunting on the former Depot have allowed the white deer to interbreed and increase in numbers for over 80 years, and along with other wildlife, roam freely within the fences.

Built at the start of World War II, the Depot was decommissioned in 2000, and authorities turned two-thirds of the 10,000-acre base over to Seneca County Industrial Development. The agency determined the best use of a 7,000-acre parcel would be a wildlife preserve called Deer Haven Park. Ninety-minute guided bus tours now take visitors along an eight-mile journey, revealing some of the mysteries of the former base. You'll follow along roadways to see powder storage buildings, personnel bunkers, a grenade range, and many of the more than 500 concrete-hardened munition igloos. Your driver will stop, and your guide will take you inside one of these mammoth structures.

While the goal of the tour is to see these elusive creatures, sightings are not guaranteed, especially since the animals are quick to use dense vegetation to remain hidden. As the bus winds its way around the complex, you might just catch a glimpse of a white deer before it darts deeper into the forest – a fleeting encounter with nature.

Address 5479 Route 96A, Romulus, NY 14541, +1 (315) 759-8220, www.deerhavenpark.org | Getting there From Geneva, take Route 20 West to Route 96A, drive 12 miles | Hours Tours & visitors center May–Oct Fri & Sat 11am–6pm (visit website for specific tour times) | Tip Nearby Sampson State Park is home to the Sampson Military Museum. Visitors are greeted by a statue that depicts a graduate, his belongings slung over his shoulder in a sea bag, waving farewell as he departs to join the war (6096 Route 96A, Romulus, NY 14541, www.parks.ny.gov).

80 Seneca Lodge

Unofficial post-race headquarters

Perched on a hill not far from Seneca Lake and a stone's throw from the breathtaking gorge in Watkins Glen State Park, this Adirondack-style lodge, steeped in local history, has been a favorite destination for vacationers, sportsmen, and racing enthusiasts since 1948. It was the very same year that the renowned Watkins Glen Grand Prix races were held, the first post-World War II road event in America. Over the decades, the Grand Prix evolved, eventually becoming part of the Formula One World Championship, attracting drivers and teams who made Seneca Lodge their unofficial post-race headquarters.

Established by Don Brubaker and carried forward by successive generations of Brubakers, the legendary lodge has evolved into a multi-faceted enterprise – 87 motel rooms and cabins, a restaurant that serves breakfast and dinner, and a one-of-a-kind tavern room, where a 1920s-era nickelodeon hums with tunes of yesteryear.

Step inside. You'll hardly believe your eyes. Walls are crammed with mementos and oddball memorabilia, each vintage, kitschy, outright bizarre object fighting for attention – newspaper clippings, college pennants, a vintage beer can collection, deer heads and photos of local hunters posing with their kills, and arrows shot into the wall, battle-scarred relics of archery tournaments. That's not all. The whole room feels like a cluttered attic, adorned with racing paraphernalia. There are flags and banners from teams and sponsors, race programs, posters, trophies, awards, and faded laurel wreaths once presented to legends like James Hunt, Jackie Stewart, and Emerson Fittipaldi following their Formula One victories.

Not quirky enough? In longstanding tradition, the bartender at Seneca Lodge hands your change back in $2 bills. There's even a special slot in the register for them – the drawer is organized to hold $1, $2, $5, $10, and $20 bills.

Address 3600 Walnut Road, Watkins Glen, NY 14891, +1 (607) 535-2014, www.senecalodge.com | Getting there From South Franklin Street in downtown Watkins Glen, take Old Corning Road (Route 17) to Walnut Road | Hours Daily from 5pm | Tip A nearby must-visit, the scenic gorge at Watkins Glen State Park features a 2-mile trail past 19 waterfalls, arched bridges, winding tunnels, and up over 800 stone steps. Wear sturdy, waterproof shoes (1009 North Franklin Street, Watkins Glen, NY 14891, www.parks.ny.gov).

81 The Seward House

He purchased Alaska for two cents an acre!

One of the region's most fascinating historical figures, William Henry Seward served as governor of New York, senator of New York, and Secretary of State, managing international affairs during the Civil War as Abraham Lincoln's "right-hand man," later serving under Ulysses Johnson. Tragically, he was stabbed as part of the conspiracy on the day Lincoln was shot, yet survived to almost single-handedly lobby for the purchase of Alaska. Today, his Auburn home stands as a museum, meticulously preserved to offer visitors a glimpse into the life and times of its illustrious inhabitant.

The Seward House is open to the public for guided tours by well-versed storytellers who share intimate details about the owner's life and achievements. It's packed with original furnishings, artifacts, portraits, and unexpected bits of history – with each room having its own story to tell.

On the night of April 14, 1865, a former Confederate soldier named Lewis Powell attacked Seward in his bed and stabbed him multiple times with a Bowie knife. The Seward House bedroom is arranged to resemble the Washington bedroom where the attack took place, displaying a swatch of blood-stained sheet, photo of the knife, a *Police Gazette* recreation of the crime, and a section of wallpaper from Ford's Theatre.

Seward believed that the Alaska territory would be strategically valuable, while critics dismissed negotiations with Russia as "Seward's Folly" and Alaska as "Seward's Ice Box." The Auburn dining room is set exactly as it was in his Washington home, where he wined, dined, and cajoled wavering congressmen into supporting the seven-million-dollar deal. Although Seward supported the abolition movement, he risked his political career by harboring fugitive slaves. The basement kitchen here is faithfully restored to resemble the original hiding place where the Sewards provided shelter and support.

Address 33 South Street, Auburn, NY 13021, +1 (315) 252-1283, www.sewardhouse.org | Getting there From downtown Auburn, follow South Street to the corner of Lincoln Street | Hours Tue–Sat 10am–5pm, Sun 1–5pm | Tip Next to the historic home, two acres of sprawling gardens are designated as Seward Park, a gift to the city by the Seward family. At its center, a bronze statue depicts Seward delivering his famous "Higher Law" speech (35 South Street, Auburn, NY 13021).

82 Shequaga Falls

From the Finger Lakes to the Louvre

Have you ever watched *Aurora Teagarden Mysteries* on the Hallmark Channel? The story is set in the fictional town of Lawrenceton, Washington, but the opening scene features a shot of one of the Finger Lakes' most iconic waterfalls.

Known as "Tumbling Waters" to the Native Americans, Shequaga Falls is a towering cascade that transforms the serene surroundings of what is now the village of Montour Falls. It starts to tumble from the arch bridge above and fans out, plunging down 156 feet of pale gray limestone and reaching a shallow basin below. The creek then continues on its way to Seneca Lake. Among the hundreds of dramatic waterfalls throughout the region, what makes this one truly notable and worth visiting is a remarkable story that originated during the late 18th century.

In 1796, Prince Louis Philippe, heir to the French throne, arrived in Philadelphia, and after attending the inauguration of John Adams, he visited Mount Vernon, home of newly retired President George Washington. When Louis expressed an interest in exploring the vast landscapes and wilderness of the young country, Washington showed him a map, marking a route that would guide him along the early American frontier.

As a royal, Louis had been tutored in painting and drawing from childhood, and it was his intention to make drawings of the places he visited. His adventure took him through the backwoods of Pennsylvania before following into the untamed Finger Lakes region, and among the many natural wonders he encountered, he was so inspired by the site of Shequaga Falls, Louis felt compelled to capture it on canvas. His sketch and later painting would survive the 1848 Revolution to eventually be housed in the Louvre Museum in Paris.

Your visit here will take you to the "Glorious T," named for the T-shaped intersection of Genesee and Main Streets, and crowned by the cascading falls.

Address 109 South Genesee Street, Montour Falls, NY 14865, www.nyfalls.com | **Getting there** From Watkins Glen, follow Route 14 to Montour Falls, turn onto North Genesee Street and follow to South Genesee Street, just past the intersection of West Main Street | **Hours** Unrestricted | **Tip** A Greek Revival home at the entrance to Shequaga Falls Park is said to be the most photographed house in New York State. It was built in 1847 by William Terry Jackson, surveyor, entrepreneur, judge, and congressman (101 North Genesee Street, Montour Falls, NY 14865).

83 Significant Elements

Everything – even the kitchen sink!

Only cats have more lives than this building, nestled in the city's Southside neighborhood. Built in 1888 for the Electric Seamless Hosiery Company, over the years it's been a carriage factory, blacksmith shop, aircraft experimental plant, corset company factory, department store warehouse, and janitorial supply retail store. In 1998, the building became home to Significant Elements, Ithaca's non-profit architectural salvage warehouse.

This unexpected place is a restoration and repurposing paradise, where every inch of three floors is crammed top to bottom with a hodgepodge of hardware and home furnishings – from columns, window frames, shutters, cabinets, doors, and woodworking tools to porcelain sinks and claw-footed bathtubs, wooden banister spindles, fireplace mantels, ornate door knobs, antique light fixtures, lamp parts and globes – all architectural wonders, each item with its own story or provenance, awaiting its next home. There's always something different, and no two visits are the same, so each day is a new opportunity to find something that speaks to you.

As a branch of Historic Ithaca, the program is committed to environmental sustainability and preservation of the city's collective cultural heritage, encouraging reclamation and reuse of building materials when the demolition of a building is inevitable. Inventory comes from recycled building materials, renovation projects, barn cleanouts, the basements and attics of supporters, and occasional demolitions – all donated by community members, contractors, businesses and institutions, with profits supporting the mission of Historic Ithaca.

Significant Elements has the distinction of being the only architectural salvage program in New York State to offer the expertise of trained, on-site preservationists, sponsor tours and lectures, and it conducts hands-on workshops and job-training programs.

Address 212 Center Street, Ithaca, NY 14850, +1 (607) 277-3450, www.significantelements.org | Getting there From downtown Ithaca, follow West Clinton Street to South Plain Street and the corner of Center Street | Hours Tue–Fri 10:30am–4pm, Sat 10am–5pm | Tip One block north on South Plain Street, the historic Southside Community Center, dedicated by First Lady Eleanor Roosevelt in 1938, provides recreation programs and employment services for the local African American community (305 South Plain Street, Ithaca, NY 14850, www.sspride.org).

84 The Six-Story Treehouse

Nature's penthouse

During the 1930s, tuberculosis was widespread in the country, and with no cure on the horizon, it was believed that placing children in fresh-air camps could prevent the disease from spreading. The Cayuga Preventorium was established here in 1939, a project of President Roosevelt's WPA. This site, overlooking Cayuga Lake, was deemed ideal for a camp that provided an abundance of fresh air and natural beauty.

In later years, the 120 acres of woodland and lodge were used for environmental education by local school districts, eventually formalized as the Cayuga Nature Center in 1981. The historic main lodge hosts exhibits focused on local forest ecology, wildlife, and climate. Educational programs offer a variety of topics, including survival, geology, ecology, and maple sugaring. Visitors can explore miles of trails with various loops that cross wooded glens and open fields along gorges and stream beds, surrounded by natural habitats.

The most popular attraction, just a five-minute walk, unmarked but directly north of the lodge, leads to an enchanting six-story treehouse, affectionately called "TreeTops," a community project, built by the Ithaca High School class of 2000, and supported by a long list of local businesses and volunteers. Cross a small footbridge to reach the base of a structure set among a cluster of trees. Adults use stairs to get to the top, while the kids enjoy climbing ladders, as they explore hidden passageways and cubby holes. The structure is fully enclosed with thousands of sticks, blending in with the forest setting and masking the protective wire.

Reaching the top, you're rewarded with a panoramic view that's both breathtaking and serene. You've ascended to a secret world, serenaded by the sound of nearby Denison Falls, named for local naturalist Marion Denison Ehrhart. The kids love it, and adults feel like kids again.

Address 1420 Taughannock Boulevard, Ithaca, NY 14850, +1 (607) 273-6260, www.cayuganaturecenter.org | Getting there From Ithaca's West End, drive north on Taughannock Boulevard (Route 89) for 5 miles | Hours Trails and treehouse open dawn to dusk, year-round | Tip Henry A. Smith Woods is a 32-acre old-growth forest left to the village of Trumansburg by Smith's sons to be preserved as a public park forever. In 2007, a loop trail was created for public hikes (8825 Falls Road, Trumansburg, NY 14886, www.cayuganaturecenture.org).

85 Skenoh Island

Native American hiding place

Located at the northwest corner of Canandaigua Lake, this small patch of land has captivated imaginations for centuries. Skenoh Island, once known as "Squaw Island," is closely tied to the history and culture of the Seneca Nation, one of the tribes of the Iroquois Confederacy. According to Seneca legend, the island was a place of refuge for Seneca women and children during a conflict with the French in the 18th century. Women of the tribe are said to have sought refuge on the island, giving it lasting cultural and historical significance.

At one time, the island was much larger. The lake's wave action has reduced its size from two acres to its present one-fifth of an acre, and Skenoh has been called "New York's smallest state park." The site came to the attention of Dr. John M. Clarke, geologist and paleontologist. It seems that Skenoh is one of only a few places worldwide where one can find rare oncolites which form in the water around the island, a geological oddity known as "water biscuits." These disc-shaped, whitish cakes of lime occur when the lime falls out of solution in the water and is deposited over small objects such as pebbles or twigs.

Today, a day trip destination, Skenoh is popular for hunting, fishing, wildlife observation, and hiking. A public boat launch is available at the north end of Canandaigua Lake State Marine Park, for trailered, motorized boats. A gently sloping concrete ramp also provides access for paddlers with car-top canoes or kayaks. Paddlers can also access the water just upstream of the boat launch at grassy areas along the creek.

In 1918, Canandaigua native Mary Clark Thompson, philanthropist and wife of prominent banker Frederick Ferris Thompson, used her influence and connections to have the island declared a New York State Museum Reservation, then arranged for the transfer on a 10-ton boulder to the island to commemorate its status.

Address Canandaigua Lake State Marine Park, 620 South Main Street, Canandaigua, NY 14424, +1 (585) 394-9420, www.parks.ny.gov | **Getting there** Follow Routes 5 & 20 or Route 332 to South Main Street | **Hours** Unrestricted | **Tip** Skenoh is not the only island in the region. Cayuga Lake has two small islands. One, near Union Springs, is uninhabited Frontenac Island, an ancient burial ground; the other is Canoga Island, just off the Canoga Marsh Wildlife Area, with 23 summer homes.

86 Smith Opera House

Saved from the wrecking ball

The majestic Smith Opera House opened on October 29, 1894, with a production of *The Count of Monte Cristo*. It starred James O'Neill, father of playwright Eugene O'Neill. The iconic red-brick, Romanesque-style theater was the dream of local philanthropist and businessman William Smith, constructed with the vision of bringing culture and entertainment to the Finger Lakes.

Over the years, the Smith has presented a wide variety of performing arts, including theater, opera, musicals, minstrel shows, burlesque, vaudeville, orchestras, bands, and singers, as well as church and memorial services, sporting events and lectures. Over its long history, shows on the Smith stage have ranged from Al Jolson getting down on his knees to sing "Mammy" and dancer Isadora Duncan shocking audiences with her bare limbs, to Bruce Springsteen and the E Street Band belting out "Blinded by the Light", plus "Piano Man" Billy Joel christening the theater's Steinway Grand.

And while it has escaped the wrecking ball more than once, the Smith survives as one of the oldest operating performing arts theaters in the United States and one of the architectural gems of the Finger Lakes. A restoration project in 1994 restored the building's exterior to its original 1894 façade, and the interior to architect Victor Rigaumount's 1931 eclectic opulence. Just as in the 1930s, today's interior design incorporates a combination of Art Deco, Spanish Baroque and Victorian influences. There are busts of Beethoven and Molière in backlit niches, a cloud machine that casts floating images, and stars that twinkle overhead, creating the illusion of a Moorish courtyard at twilight.

The Smith features a variety of live performances year-round, and on weekends, the theater shows movies on the region's largest indoor movie screen. Visitors are welcome to view the historic interior during regular business hours.

Address 82 Seneca Street, Geneva, NY 14456, +1 (315) 781-5483, www.thesmith.org | **Getting there** Entering Geneva on Routes 5 & 20, turn onto South Main Street, then onto Seneca Street | **Hours** Tue–Fri 10am–12:30pm and 1:30–4pm; free history tours Wed 10am during summer hours | **Tip** Another Victor Rigaumount project, Ithaca's historic State Theatre is an example of "Collegiate Gothic," a popular design in American college towns from 1900 through the 1930s (107 West State Street, Ithaca, NY 148650, www.stateofithaca.org).

87 Smoke-Breathing Dragon

Puff, the Cortland dragon

Established in 1868 to train teachers for the growing public school system, the Cortland Normal School became part of New York State's teacher education system. It was 1933, and the school's athletic teams, known as the "Normals," needed a better nickname. It fell to a resourceful team manager, inspired by the flying-red-horse trademark of Mobil gas stations, who suggested "Red Dragons."

In 1941, the institution became known as Cortland State Teachers College, and with the founding of the SUNY system, in 1961, renamed SUNY College at Cortland. Throughout the school's evolution, the Red Dragon has remained a symbol of identity within the school's athletic programs, including a cheerleading mascot actor dressed in a dragon costume. In 2017, two Cortland grads joined forces to provide the dragon a permanent home on campus. Financed by Mike Vela '88 and handcrafted by Scott Oldfield '06, a towering, 15-foot-tall, smoke-breathing sculpture, unveiled on Homecoming Weekend, now guards the entrance to the stadium complex.

Oldfield, now a lecturer in Cortland's Art and Art History Department, crafted the behemoth based on the dragon logo, translating a two-dimensional image into a three-dimensional, stainless-steel sculpture. Beginning with a one-twentieth-scale model, approved by committee, the six-month project included initial staging, sourcing materials, fabricating the infrastructure, crafting and attaching drop-swoop wings, installing a smoke machine, and painting the creature in official school red. The sculpture's intricate details include piercing eyes, sharp teeth, elongated tail, and claws gripping firmly onto the base.

The school's facilities team installed the concrete base and completed the electrical wiring necessary to power the smoke-breathing mechanism – the dragon lets out a mighty plume of smoke whenever the home team scores. Go Red Dragons!

Address 17 Lankler Drive, Cortland, NY 13045, +1 (607) 753-2011, www2.cortland.edu | Getting there From Route 281 (West Road), turn onto Lankler Drive | Hours Unrestricted | Tip "Touchdown," the Big Red Bear, is the unofficial mascot of Cornell University, once a live bear, now a bronze statue across from Schoellkopf Field. Players rub the bear's head for luck before home football games (513 Campus Road, Ithaca, NY 14853).

88 Sonnenberg's Secret Garden

Taking tea with the Thompsons

If you're a fan of the fictional Yorkshire country estate of Downton Abbey and the aristocratic Crawley family, you'll recognize this example of Victorian-Edwardian lifestyle in the Finger Lakes, the summer home of Frederick Ferris Thompson and his wife, Mary Clark Thompson. He was a prominent New York banker and railroad president who co-founded the First National Bank (what is now Citibank). She was the daughter of Myron H. Clark, the governor of New York. Today, their wealth and privilege is on display at the "Grand Dame of Canandaigua."

While many of their upper-crust friends had summer homes on Long Island or along the Hudson River Valley, the Thompsons built "Sonnenberg" (German for "sunny hill"), a baronial, 3-story, 40-room, Queen Anne-style mansion in the town where Mary grew up, its design influenced by the most popular architecture of the Gilded Age. Major rooms include the grand dining room, trophy room, billiard room, library, circular rotunda, and the wood-paneled, medieval-style, two-story Great Hall.

A passionate gardener, Mary commissioned the creation of nine formal gardens on the 52-acre estate, including a serene Japanese garden with a pond and a tea house, a colorful Italian garden with statues and fountains, and a fragrant rose garden with more than 2,500 varieties of roses. Perhaps most interesting is the Sub-Rosa or "Secret Garden," enclosed by a circle of tall, lush hedges, a secluded setting where the Thompsons hosted afternoon tea for their guests. You can almost picture women in elegant hats and summer dresses, men in tailored blazers and straw boater hats, and hear silver spoons clinking against porcelain cups.

Not to be missed on a self-guided tour of the estate is the 13,000-square-foot conservatory complex, designed by Lord & Burnham of New York City, one of the most important residential greenhouses in the United States.

Address 250 Gibson Street, Canandaigua, NY 14424, +1 (585) 394-4922, www.sonnenberg.org | Getting there From downtown Canandaigua, take North Main Street to Gibson Street | Hours May–Oct Thu–Mon 9:30am–4:30pm | Tip A sculpture by Dexter Benedict of Penn Yan honors Mary Lee Clark Thompson for her gift of the F. F. Thompson Hospital in memory of her husband Frederick Ferris Thompson (350 Parrish Street, Canandaigua, NY 14424).

89 Stubby's Locomotive

Hot dogs off the rails

The Finger Lakes Railway is a short-line freight railroad headquartered in Geneva. It runs on legacy tracks from the New York Central and Lehigh Valley railroads, passing through town *en route* between Syracuse and Canandaigua. Don't blink as you drive along the lakefront and past lines of freight cars or you'll miss the tiny, eight-foot by ten-foot, vintage railroad structure, fashioned from the cab of a 1941 diesel locomotive that enjoyed a long service life on the Rock Island Line. For anyone who's not sure what to make of it, or for that matter, anyone who doesn't believe their eyes, the playful name "Stubby's" explains the diminutive size.

This eccentric eatery is the brainchild of Gerry Collins, a man with an obsession that sets him apart. He's been infatuated with the thrill of transforming the forgotten, the out-of-place, or the downright wacky into places where people gather to eat, laugh, and linger. He once reworked a metal shed into the "World's Smallest Diner."

There's barely enough room for Gerry, chief cook and bottle washer, a refrigerator and a four-foot grill inside. The menu includes a classic cheeseburger and a choice of over-the-top hot dogs. The Coney Island hot dog is topped with a savory meat sauce, mustard, and chopped raw onions, and it comes with the story about the Greek immigrants who developed this combination in the early 1900s. Other versions include the spicy Poncho Villa, the coleslaw-smothered Southern Belle, and a mustard, relish, onion, and sauerkraut-topped "classic."

Every Thursday through Sunday, nearly all year round, curious tourists who flock into Geneva are drawn to this oddity, and while there are no booths or counter, no jukebox or waitstaff, this gathering spot, nestled in the heart of a small American town, is an honest mix of nourishment and nostalgia.

Address 41 Lake Street, Geneva, NY 14456 | **Getting there** Entering the city of Geneva on Routes 5 & 20, turn onto Lake Street | **Hours** Thu–Sun, 10am–8pm | **Tip** Next door to Stubby's, a former 1920s Texaco gas station, built in West Coast-inspired, Spanish Colonial style, is now the Lake Street Station Wine Bar, a place where you can still fill 'er up, only now with tasty beverages (41 Lake Street, Geneva, NY 14456).

90 The Sundae's Birthplace

The city with a cherry on top

More than any other native dish, ice cream sundaes are essential reminders of the American genius for invention, passion for indulgence, and reputation for wackiness. From hot-fudge sundaes and tin-roof sundaes to brownie-bottom sundaes and banana splits – they have become the most ubiquitous desserts in America, inspiring countless imitations worldwide.

There's a modest marker, set in the Ithaca Commons sidewalk, but it memorializes a significant event that happened at this spot, once the home of the Platt & Colt Pharmacy. On Sunday, April 3, 1892, Reverend John M. Scott delivered a sermon at the Unitarian Church, then paid a visit to the pharmacy fountain for his usual dish of vanilla ice cream, but on that day, proprietor Chester Platt added cherry syrup and placed a candied cherry at the top. After some debate, Scott suggested that it be named for the day it was created. Platt concurred and the "Cherry Sunday" was born.

The new dish gained widespread popularity as Cornell University students, returning to their hometowns across the country, introduced it to local fountains. By the turn of the century (and with a change in spelling that distinguished the dessert from the Sabbath), ice cream sundaes were being served nationwide. And although several other cities have challenged the Ithaca story, an *Ithaca Journal* advertisement for Platt & Colt's "new ten-cent specialty," dated April 5, 1892, provides irrefutable evidence, the oldest-known record of the sundae's invention.

The Platt & Colt Pharmacy is gone, but Ithacans find many places in town to enjoy sundaes, most notably the Purity Ice Cream Company, founded in 1936 by Leo Guentert who studied dairy science at Cornell, then worked for the Nestle Company before returning to Ithaca to set out on his own. He called his ice cream shop "Purity" to reflect the strict hygienic standards he had learned at Cornell.

Address 216 East State Street, Ithaca Commons, Ithaca, NY 14850, www.cityofithaca.org | Getting there Follow Route 79 into Ithaca and continue on State Street into downtown | Hours Unrestricted | Tip The Dairy Bar in Stocking Hall on the Cornell campus is home of "educated ice cream," where students from the Food Science Department devise ways to craft premium ice cream flavors in small batches (411 Tower Road, Ithaca, NY 14853, www.sci.cornell.edu/cornell-dairy-bar).

91__The Sutton Company

Home of the legendary "spoons"

In 1867, a local Naples jeweler and avid fisherman by the name of Scott R. Sutton began making hand-pressed, copper and brass, silver-plated fishing lures. It was the birth of the Sutton Company.

Spoon-style lures have long been favored by anglers for their ability to attract a wide variety of fish species. Named for their resemblance to a dinner table spoon's concave shape, these lures have a curved, oval design that creates a fluttering motion in the water that mimics the movement of fish, and the shiny, metallic surface of the spoon reflects light, attracting fish to a hook attached to the rear of the spoon. The legendary Sutton Spoon has endured for generations, and over three generations of Staffords – Jack Stafford, who purchased the business in 1929, Jim Stafford, and currently, Deirdre Stafford Stevenson, who is devoted to carrying forward the Sutton legacy.

It's not surprising that an iconic lure originated here. Naples Creek offers some of the finest freshwater fishing in the region, with rainbow trout runs that draw anglers here each spring. Since 1944, the lures have been made by hand in this remarkable shop on the village Main Street, and stepping inside tells you not much has changed since the 1940s. The floors are wooden, worn smooth from decades of footsteps. Shelves and tables are lined and stacked with all manner of fishing gear – rods, reels, tackle, nets, hats, boots, and, of course, the lures.

Sutton Spoons are made in a wide range of types and sizes for a variety of trolling and casting, referred to by number. Beginning with 50-pound copper and brass coils, a multi-step process begins with a hydraulic punch press and finishes with silver plating. Deirdre explains that "passion and love are infused into each handcrafted spoon," while the enterprise remains old-school, relying strictly on brand loyalty and word of mouth.

Address 120 South Main Street, Naples, NY 14512, +1 (585) 374-2628 | **Getting there** Route 21 (along the west side of Canandaigua Lake) becomes Main Street in Naples | **Hours** Mon–Sat 9am–5:30pm | **Tip** Rainbow trout typically move out of the Finger Lakes in late winter and early spring to spawn in various feeder streams such as Naples Creek. There's some good angling in these tributaries when the trout season officially opens on April 1.

92 Taughannock Falls

Taller than Niagara

In 1869, English daredevil Andrew Jenkens, who called himself "The Professor," crossed Niagara Falls on a four-inch-diameter rope, pedaling a contraption named the "doon bike," resembling a bicycle turned upside down, and instead of tires, its wide wheels had deep grooves designed to glide along the rope. Five years later, Jenkens performed the same stunt over the tallest, free-falling, single-drop waterfall in the Northeast. Taughannock (pronounced *tuck-han'-uck*), whose 215-foot vertical drop is 33 feet higher than iconic Niagara Falls, plunges through a rock amphitheater framed by towering gorge walls reaching to 400 feet.

While there have been several documented leaps over Niagara Falls – with a mix of both success and tragedy – the only person known to have gone over Taughannock gave the falls its name. According to legend, during a battle over territorial sovereignty between Native American tribes, the Delaware (Lenape), who first occupied this region, and Cayugas of the Iroquois Confederacy, Delaware chief Taghkanic was thrown over the falls after the defeat of his warriors.

There are a few ways to view and experience majestic Taughannock Falls. The Overlook provides a stunning, unobstructed view from above, easily accessible by car. Rim trails offer an elevated perspective of the gorge and the falls; the North Rim Trail provides views of the gorge and the falls from above, while the South Rim Trail offers panoramic views of Cayuga Lake and the surrounding area.

For the most immersive experience, hike the Gorge Trail along Taughannock Creek. It's lined with diverse plant life and towering rock walls rising on either side, creating a dramatic natural corridor leading to the base of the cascading waters. As you draw nearer, the towering height and fierce power of the falls become even more awe-inspiring, especially at their fullest during spring thaw.

Address 2381 Taughannock Park Road, Trumansburg, NY 14886, +1 (607) 387-6739, www.parks.ny.gov | Getting there From Route 95, turn onto Taughannock Park Road, and follow signs to the Overlook | Hours Unrestricted (trails are icy in winter) | Tip Ithaca has over 150 waterfalls within a 10-mile radius of downtown. Among the most dramatic is thundering Lucifer Falls in Robert Treman State Park (known locally as Enfield Glen) with a 115-foot drop (129 Upper Park Road, Ithaca, NY 14850).

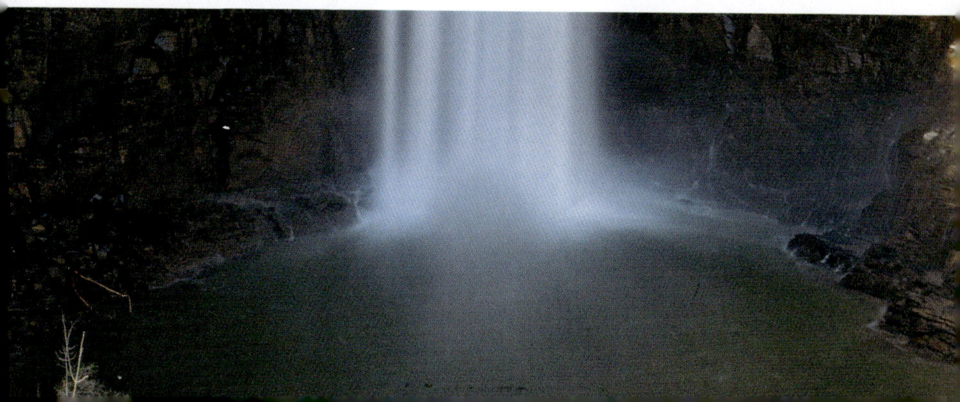

93 The Taughannock Giant

The "giant" hoax of 1879

John Thompson, owner of a hotel near the Taughannock Falls overlook, fashioned himself after showman and promoter P. T. Barnum. He once hired Andrew "The Professor" Jenkins, a Canadian daredevil, to cross the gorge on a tightrope. In the summer of 1879, in a plan to attract publicity, as well as guests to the hotel, he orchestrated a hoax worthy of the great Barnum. Along with two collaborators, Thompson mixed a compound of cement, iron filings, organic materials, and plaster, molded the material into the shape of a human-like creature, and secretly buried it near a construction site on the hotel grounds.

Workers eventually uncovered what appeared to be the contorted body of an ancient, petrified man, with hands crossed over his right thigh, and left leg crossed over the right, frozen in time. News of the discovery took hold, newspapers picked up the story, and thousands of spectators were drawn to the scene. Thompson set up a tent over the excavation, charging 10 cents for admission to view the "Taughannock Giant." Ultimately, the get-rich-quick scheme was debunked, and the story faded into folklore – until 2019.

That year, folks at the Tompkins County History Center received a grant to memorialize the archaeological scam, providing funds for local artist Annemarie Zwack to create a true-to-scale reproduction of the "stone man." She was able to study old newspaper photos taken after the discovery and, working with blacksmiths Durand Van Doren and Teo Aceto, designed an armature, the sturdy metal framework that was filled with concrete and sculpted to replicate the piece with historical accuracy.

The replica giant was on display in Ithaca before being moved to a permanent home under a small pavilion in Trumansburg. The hoax is commemorated on a marker at the site, recounting the tale with a bit of humor, and sharing the quirky local legacy.

Address Opposite the intersection of Route 227 and Route 96, Trumansburg, NY 14886, www.trumansburg.ny.gov | **Getting there** From the village of Trumansburg, drive north on West Main Street (Route 96) to the intersection of Hector Road (Route 227) | **Hours** Unrestricted | **Tip** Nearby Black Diamond Farm is the home of Ian Merwin, one of the most influential mentors in the community of American cider makers. Stop by to taste ciders and learn about the cidermaking process (4675 East Seneca Road, Trumansburg, NY 14886, www.blackdiamondcider.com).

94 Teal Park Bandstand

Cartoon character creation

When Swiss-born Eugene Zimmerman stepped off the boat in New York Harbor in 1868, he had no idea that his doodles would one day capture the hearts of millions and transform him into the celebrated cartoonist known worldwide as "Zim." While working as a sign painter, he copied the work of the era's cartoonists, eventually developing a style of his own. After showing his portfolio to Joseph Keppler, director of *Puck* magazine, he was hired on the spot.

In 1885, he dropped the last portion of his signature to become "Zim," producing works that ranged from simple pencil drawings to lifelike paintings. His biting sense of humor propelled him to the top of his field, while the magazine became a powerful platform for social and political commentary, targeting corruption, hypocrisy, and various societal issues. After two and a half years at *Puck*, Zim was persuaded to move to *Judge*, the rival satirical magazine. A pioneer in the field of caricature and comic strips, during his lifetime, Zim produced tens of thousands of gags, caricatures, and illustrations.

In 1888, in search of a more gentle pace of life, he galloped away from New York City to the village of Horseheads, traveling back to the city on alternate weeks to fulfill commitments at the magazine. He became a volunteer fireman in the village, drew caricatures of local businessmen and friends, and as an amateur musician, he designed and led the effort to build an outdoor bandstand in Teal Park. As the "Z Band," he and a small group of friends serenaded villagers at special events.

The ornamental, gazebo-like bandstand includes a comical fiddling frog carving, an example of Zim's "animal antics," one of his favorite themes. Today, as one of the town's cultural points of pride, the bandstand hosts free concerts in the park every Thursday evening from Memorial Day to Labor Day. Bring lawn chairs.

Address 500 South Main Street, Horseheads, NY 14845, +1 (607) 739-5691, www.horseheads.org | **Getting there** Follow Route 13 to the intersection with I-86. Follow signs to Route 14 and drive directly into Horseheads and onto Main Street in the center of the village | **Hours** Unrestricted | **Tip** The nearby home of Eugene Zimmerman, the legendary cartoonist known as "Zim," now serves as a museum, showcasing his papers, sketches, and mementos (601 North Pine Street, Horseheads, NY 14845; to schedule a tour, email horseheadshistoricalsociety@yahoo.com).

95 Teddy Roosevelt's Tree

In memory of his fallen comrade

During the American intervention in the Cuban War of Independence, a volunteer cavalry composed of cowboys, miners, law-enforcement officers, and Ivy League athletes, nicknamed the "Rough Riders," were commanded by Lieutenant Colonel Theodore Roosevelt. On July 1, 1898, Roosevelt led a series of charges up San Juan Hill on his horse, Texas, while his men followed on foot. The attack was a success, defeating the Spanish defenders, despite suffering many casualties.

Among those who dropped their studies at Cornell to join the Rough Riders was 22-year-old architecture student Clifton Beckwith Brown. Tasked with capturing a low ridge on the hill, Brown's unit took heavy incoming fire while moving against a hilltop bunker. As he cut through barbed wire, a Spanish bullet pierced his skull, killing Brown instantly. Out of 490 Rough Riders who participated in the battle, eight men were killed, and more than 80 were wounded during the assault. Brown became the first Cornellian to give his life for his country.

The story of Roosevelt and the Rough Riders was celebrated by newspapers and popular songs, and in the wake of his war-hero status, Roosevelt secured the Republican gubernatorial nomination, and was elected governor of New York on November 8, 1898.

During his time as a student at Harvard, Roosevelt was a member of the Delta Kappa Epsilon fraternity, and on a trip to Ithaca a year after taking office, the governor paid a visit to the "Deke" chapter house at Cornell for a ceremony honoring his fraternity brother, fallen comrade Clifton Beckwith Brown, planting two Norway spruce evergreens at a corner of the grounds. Over the years, the one remaining tree has grown taller than the spire on the castle-like building, among the university's oldest fraternity houses. Beneath the historic tree, a weathered marker, fixed on a granite stone, tells the remarkable story.

Address 13 South Avenue, Ithaca, NY 14850, www.dke-cornell.org | Getting there From Route 79, heading east out of downtown Ithaca, take Stewart Avenue to Campus Road, then turn onto South Avenue | Hours Unrestricted | Tip A bronze bas-relief in honor of Clifton Beckwith Brown, sculpted by Bela Lyon Pratt, is mounted on the east wall of the Hartell Gallery in Cornell's Sibley Dome (921 University Avenue, Ithaca, NY 14853).

96 The Three Bears of Ovid

Mama, Papa, and Baby Greek Revivals

Everyone knows about Goldilocks and the three bears – the great big father bear, a middle-sized mother bear, and pint-sized baby bear. Three sequentially scaled Greek Revival-style buildings that make up the former courthouse complex in the Seneca County village of Ovid remind local folks of the timeless fairy tale.

Once upon a time – actually in 1845 – two of the three brick buildings were constructed. The largest, "Papa Bear," became the county courthouse with a stone jail in the cellar, and the smallest, "Baby Bear," housed the county clerk's office. Architect Obadiah B. Latham adhered to the prevailing Greek Revival tradition for significant government buildings, a style that conveyed stability and authority. In 1859, it was decided that the county clerk needed more space to store records and a third building, "Mama Bear," was erected in between Papa and Baby. The arrangement of these graduated, storybook-like structures on Ovid's sloping hillside park is unique in the United States, and now listed on the National Registry of Historic Places. Nowhere else will you find a comparable assembly of Greek Revival public buildings standing side-by-side.

Mama Bear has become the Seneca County tourist center. You're welcome to stop in to learn about other Finger Lake attractions. Walk the stairs to see maps of the village, town, and county. Baby Bear is home to the Sons of Union Veterans of the Civil War, but Papa is the most interesting Bear.

There's a draconian, three-cell jail in the basement. The first floor, which once housed the sheriff's office, living quarters, and jury room, now has the original clerk's desk and jury deliberation table on display. The second floor contains the old county courtroom, meticulously preserved to look just as it did in the 19th century, with George Washington's portrait surrounded by judges who once presided here.

Address 7175 North Main Street, Ovid, NY 14521, +1 (607) 869-3818, www.threebearsovid.org | **Getting there** At the intersection of Routes 96, 96A, and 414, follow Route 414 south into the village of Ovid | **Hours** Thu–Sat 10am–2pm, Sun noon–2pm | **Tip** The Ovid Free Library was housed in "Mama Bear" from 1905 until 1962, when books were moved via bucket brigade to the new library, a New Formalist-style building, donated by mathematician Walter Burton Ford in honor of his wife Edith (7169 Main Street, Ovid, NY 14521, www.ovidlibrary.org).

97 Twisted Rail Brewing

The last pitcher show

With two dozen different beers on tap, this is the epitome of a kid-in-a-candy-store for beer nerds, or you could say, kid-in-a-movie theater.

The enterprise began in 2013 as a humble three-barrel microbrewery housed in part of an old railroad depot in Canandaigua. Efforts of the beer-mad trio of Ian Boni, John McMullen and Rich Russ have paid off, and over recent years, Twisted Rail has established outpost tasting rooms in Honeoye, Macedon, and the original Canandaigua location with the mothership brewhouse now headquartered here in the former Regent Theatre building.

A new form of entertainment swept into Geneva in 1915, when the Regent opened on Exchange Street, boasting an elaborate interior adorned with chandeliers, plush seating, and ornate decorations. Opening day attracted a turn-away crowd to see Charlie Chaplin in *The Tramp* with a live pianist playing music to accompany the film. Newspaper accounts described the visual experience as "mesmerizing" to many folks who had never seen anything like it before. During the Great Depression, the theatre, like many other businesses in town, was forced to close its doors. It reopened in the early 1940s as part of the Schine Circuit chain, but closed again during the 1950s. Many years later, the building was repurposed to house a church congregation.

There is still abundant evidence of the theatre's past life: a massive chandelier in the lobby, stained glass windows, gold-painted balcony, crown molding, movie poster marquees, and the original ticket booth. But now a 20-barrel brewhouse is at center stage, and craft beers are the feature attraction. Begin your visit here with a pour of easy-drinking Lake to Lake Lager. Follow that up with Spike Driver, the flagship IPA. In winter, the Chocolate Espresso Stout, with its roasted coffee aroma, is as good a way as any to ward off chilly lake breezes.

Address 499 Exchange Street, Geneva, NY 14456, +1 (315) 325-6995, www.twistedrailbrewing.com | Getting there Downtown Geneva, on Exchange Street, just east of Franklin Street | Hours Mon–Thu 11:30am–9pm, Fri & Sat 11am–10pm, Sun noon–6pm | Tip Opened in 1924, and still showing movies after all these years, the Glen Theater in Watkins Glen is a cherished local landmark (112 North Franklin Street, Watkins Glen, NY 14891).

98 Unique Toy Shop

Reconnect with your inner child

Main Street in Canandaigua features stately homes, distinguished civic buildings, historic churches, and handsome commercial structures. A portion of the bustling four-lane avenue is beautified by a grassy median, while the business district is lined with wide, welcoming sidewalks. A local treasure in the heart of downtown since 1983, the Unique Toy Shop has a sign above the door that reads "Discover Play" and beckons passersby with brightly colored displays in the store windows.

This is a woman-owned, women-run business. Behind the counter, you'll meet Katy McCarthy-Hodock, or perhaps one of her three daughters. Laura, Mary, and Libby all lend a hand, warmly greeting customers; they know many by name. The store is a throwback to the days when parents and grandparents could shop without the rush of modern life, taking their time to pick out toys that would last and be loved for years.

More than just a place to purchase playthings, its name was chosen with purpose. The thoughtfully curated selections, vintage play areas, and personalized shopping experience make this a truly unique destination, setting it apart as a one-of-a-kind toy store in the region.

Inside the twin storefronts, shelves are packed to the brim with toys for children and grown-ups who don't want to grow up – every corner is a reminder of an earlier time. The shop specializes in hard-to-find, non-electronic toys, an array of items rarely seen in the mass market. From dress-up kits to traditional, classic, vintage, and retro toys you thought were gone forever, as well as timeless toys and games for kids of all ages, infant to adult – puppets and dolls, books and art supplies, puzzles and models, magic tricks, wooden toys, active-play toys. And don't miss an inviting corner in the back of the shop with an array of stuffed toys in every imaginable size, color, and shape.

Address 120 South Main Street, Canandaigua, NY 14424, +1 (585) 394-2319, www.uniquetoyshop.com | Getting there From Routes 5 & 20, turn onto South Main Street | Hours Mon–Sat 10am–5pm, Sun noon–4pm | Tip Further down Main Street, stop for breakfast or lunch at the oldest continuously operated restaurant in the region. Originally opened as the "Railroad Lunch" in 1892, serving hungry travelers near the New York Central Railroad station, Patty's Place continues to dish out comfort food (33 South Main Street, Canandaigua, NY 14424, www.pattysplacediner.com).

99_Walter Taylor's Goat

Wine country's greatest showman

It's hard to overstate the eccentricity of Bully Hill. The winery, situated on a terraced hillside overlooking Keuka Lake, is the inspiration and creation of a charismatic showman, who turned disdain for his family's business into one of the most interesting destinations in the Finger Lakes. Bully Hill's founder, Walter S. Taylor, was a larger-than-life character, the grandson of the founder of the Taylor Wine Company, and an eager provocateur. He railed against the "wine factory" the company had become by the time it was swallowed up by Coca-Cola in 1977.

A Barnum-like ability to capture public attention came naturally to Walter. After all, he was a distant cousin of Phineas Taylor (P. T.) Barnum, the man who built a circus empire with outrageous promotion and guile. When Coke enjoined him from using the family name on the labels of his own wines, he started calling himself "Walter S. Blank." A talented artist, he drew his own irreverent label with an image of a billy goat and the slogan, "They have my name and my heritage, but they didn't get my goat." And as an attention-grabbing stunt, Walter painted the word "Taylor" on a live goat, paraded it through Hammondsport, and dropped it off at the Taylor Wine Company's front door.

While the rascally firebrand is gone from his winery, the memory of his greatest battle is commemorated by a remarkable sculpture that greets visitors to the estate. It's an iconic, larger-than-life, bronze and copper goat – at its side, Walter's signature Havana hat – a work by Hammondsport artist Tony Moretti called *Love My Goat*.

Walk upstairs behind the sculpture to visit the cooper shop, a wine barrel exhibit, then next door to the Taylor family wine museum collection, devoted to the history of the local wine industry, with an adjoining art gallery, featuring nearly 150 of Walter's original paintings on permanent display.

Address 8843 Greyton H Taylor Memorial Drive, Hammondsport, NY 14840, +1 (607) 868-3610, www.bullyhillvineyards.com | Getting there From the village of Hammondsport, follow Pulteney Street to Greyton H Taylor Memorial Drive | Hours Daily 10am–5pm | Tip Located at the southern tip of Keuka Lake, Hammondsport is the home of Pleasant Valley Wine Company, the first winery in the region and the first bonded winery in the country (8260 Pleasant Valley Road, Hammondsport, NY 14840, www.pleasantvalleywine.com).

100 Ward O'Hara's Museum

Small town version of the Smithsonian

It all began with Ward O'Hara, gentleman farmer, John Deere farm implement dealer, newspaper columnist, and inveterate collector of farming equipment and farmhouse memorabilia. When the personal collection outgrew his home in Aurelius, he persuaded the Cayuga County Legislature to transform the old pavilion at Emerson Park in Auburn into an agricultural museum, showcasing the evolution of farming practices, machinery, and rural life. Opened to the public as the County Museum in 1975, it was renamed the Ward W. O'Hara Agricultural Museum in 1997.

At the entrance there's a photo of Mr. O'Hara in an Irish flat cap and a display of every John Deere tractor in miniature. Follow along to view hand tools such as plows, scythes, and sickles used by early farmers. A large portion of the museum is dedicated to the display of historical farm machinery, including horse-drawn plows, threshers, tilling equipment, harvesting equipment, and a room filled with tractors of every shape and size. There are themed areas focusing on everyday rural life artifacts, farming household items, old photographs of Main Streets, and full-scale replicas, including a farm kitchen, schoolhouse classroom, blacksmith and woodworking shop, and mortise and tenon barn.

A country store mercantile exhibit has a post office mail sorter and a vintage Toledo counter scale and is stocked with everything from coffee mill and old coffee cans to top hats, straw hats, and bonnets. You'll also see countless objects of rural American life, including antique pianos, radios, gramophones, Victrolas, sleds, sleighs, buggies, and a milk delivery truck. There's an enchanting dollhouse display and a circus-themed room overflowing with a stunning collection in miniature.

Allow at least an hour or so to browse through the museum, and don't miss Ward O'Hara's own 1927 Ford Model T touring convertible on display.

Address 6880 East Lake Road (Route 38A), Auburn, NY 13021, +1 (315) 252-7644, www.wardwoharaagriculturalmuseum.org | Getting there From Route 20, turn onto Owasco Road/East Lake Road (across from Emerson Park) | Hours Mon–Fri 9am–5pm, Sat & Sun 11am–3pm | Tip CNY Living History Center is made up of three different museums – military and local history, the Brockway truck museum, and the Tractors of Yesteryear museum (4386 Route 11, Cortland, NY 13045, www.cnylivinghistory.org).

101 Washington's Portrait

An original – almost

At the Louvre Museum, the first painting most visitors want to see is the *Mona Lisa*. At the Rose Hill Mansion in Geneva, the main attraction is a portrait of George Washington – mostly because it comes with a story.

The sprawling property was first developed as a farm in 1802 by Robert Selden Rose, agriculturalist and US Congressman, and in 1839, William Kerley Strong, a wealthy wool merchant, bought the land and built the mansion. Twelve years later, Benjamin Swan bought the mansion and property for his son, Robert, as a wedding gift. After Robert's death in 1890, the estate was bought and sold eight times over the next 70 years, before repurchase by descendants of the Swan family. In 1965, Waldo Hutchins Jr., grandson of Robert Swan, donated the estate to the Geneva Historical Society, and Rose Hill Mansion was opened to the public in 1968.

The National Park Service declared the estate a National Historic Landmark in 1986, calling it "one of the finest examples of the Greek Revival style in the United States." Built on a monumental scale, it reflects the prosperity of Western New York as a result of the Erie Canal. Today, guided tours focus on the Swan family's life and times in the stately home. Twenty-one meticulously furnished and period-decorated rooms are open to the public, including the back parlor, where you'll get to see that intriguing portrait of George Washington.

While it was not done by portraitist Gilbert Stuart, whose 1796 portrait of Washington is on the face of the one-dollar bill, the portrait at Rose Hill was the work of Stuart's youngest child, Jane Stuart. She often worked on and later copied portraits made by her father, and this painting of Washington exhibited her skill as an artist, capturing light and depicting true facial features and expression. Her painting was so skillful that it's often confused with her father's original.

Address 3373 Route 96A, Geneva, NY 14456, +1 (315) 789-3848, www.historicgeneva.org | Getting there From Geneva, take Route 20 east to Route 96A for half a mile | Hours Grounds open year-round during daylight hours; Mansion open May–Oct Tue–Sat 10am–4pm, Sun noon–4pm (guided tours only) | Tip The Carriage House Gift Shop features a selection of locally produced food products, historically themed gifts, and handcrafted items. A restored 1916 Model T that belonged to a descendant of the Swan family is on display.

102__Wayne's World

A man and his passions

He calls himself a country bumpkin, but Wayne Myers is better described as a visionary artisan, master builder, solo craftsman, historian, and collector. Classes in landscape architecture and greenhouse production during his studies as a Cornell Aggie prepared him for a nearly half-century personal project, transforming his family homestead into a living storybook.

Driven by an inherited passion for gardens, from both his mother and grandmother, he has a deep appreciation for the natural beauty of stone, and is in relentless pursuit of rare and remarkable things. Wayne immersed himself in an extraordinary solo endeavor that has become something of an unofficial tourist attraction. The sign out front reads "Myers' Garden," and while his six acres of rolling lawn include over 600 different perennials in a sculpture park of fieldstone walls, this place is more than just a garden. In fact, local folks call it "Wayne's World."

The unexpected wonders of his fantasy world include a collection of 1,500 fire bricks and paving bricks. Display racks in a pergola near the house include mostly pre-1940 branded bricks, emblazoned with names of companies and towns around the country. Other sections of the homestead contain a jaw-dropping 30-foot sundial with a 7-foot gnomon on a terrace built from over 50 tons of stone. There's an octagonal gazebo, a hand-built pond, a covered bridge over a creek, and a working waterwheel.

The garden has grown into a miniature village, complete with a gristmill, feed mill, cider house, wagon shed housing an 1860s-era horse-drawn carriage, and blacksmith shop filled with antique tools and implements. And don't miss the restored outhouse, an original three-holer.

The magic here is mostly the man himself. He enjoys personally guiding visitors through his village, sharing stories and the inspiration behind each structure and each collection.

Address 1071 Michigan Hollow Road, Spencer, NY 14883, +1 (607) 589-4572 | Getting there From Ithaca, follow Route 96B to Michigan Hollow Road, follow to the intersection of Hillview Road | Hours By appointment only | Tip The Elizabeth Mulholland Wildflower Preserve along Six Mile Creek in Ithaca is a nature park with trails, waterfalls, rock formations, and wildlife viewing (501-03 Giles Street, Ithaca, NY 14850).

103 Wharton Brothers Studio

They made movies in Ithaca

When brothers Theo and Leo Wharton arrived in Ithaca to film a Cornell football game for the Essanay Film Company, they found the iconic gorges perfect for thrilling stunts in serials and features. In April of 1914, they leased a former dance pavilion on the southernmost shore of Cayuga Lake in Ithaca, where they produced more than 100 films of the silent era.

The term "cliffhanger" comes from the weekly serial episodes in which a heroine would end up hanging over a cliff as a villain waited for her to plummet to her death. Theater audiences would need to return the following week to find out how the heroine escaped. The most popular Wharton serials were *The Exploits of Elaine*, starring Pearl White, and *Patria,* starring Irene Castle, both female protagonists, variously chased, rescued, and wooed. Other early movie stars who worked here included Lionel Barrymore, Francis X. Bushman, Beverly Bayne, Warner Oland (later gaining fame as "Charlie Chan") and Oliver Hardy (before teaming with Stan Laurel).

For a few fleeting years, Ithaca was the epicenter of America's burgeoning motion picture industry. Unfortunately, shooting units began searching for locations that offered consistent, year-round sunshine, and Southern California emerged as a better choice. After the Whartons headed west, the City of Ithaca purchased the movie studio property for use as a public park, named in honor of Mayor Edwin Stewart.

On a visit here, you can imagine a place once filled with chaos and creativity – a director barking instructions to actors and set designers, cameramen cranking cameras by hand. Yet for most of the past century, the studio has been a forgotten relic, used mainly for storage and restrooms. Fortunately, efforts are underway to restore the building as a cultural landmark, preserving its legacy and honoring the city's role in the early history of film.

Address 1 James L Gibbs Drive, Ithaca, NY 14850, www.whartonstudiomuseum.org | Getting there Take the Route 34 exit off Route 13 and turn onto James L Gibbs Drive | Hours Daily 8am–10pm | Tip While filming *Patria,* movie star Irene Castle met Robert Elias Treman of the Ithaca Tremans. After the two were married, they settled into an estate called "Greystone" and had the swimming pool filled with salt water from Atlantic City. It's now the Sigma Chi fraternity house (106 Cayuga Heights Road, Ithaca, NY 14850).

104 Wilder Brain Collection

The "brainchild" of a Civil War surgeon

Uris Hall on the Cornell University campus not only houses the Departments of Economics, Sociology, Gender Studies, and Psychology, but – yikes! – the brain of one of the most notorious criminals of the 19th century. If you're sure you're ready to visit, take the elevator to the second floor to view the slightly ghoulish exhibit of human brains, eight of the sixty surviving specimens in a collection begun by Burt Green Wilder, a former Civil War surgeon and one of Cornell's original faculty members.

It was Dr. Wilder who formally established the Cornell Brain Society, a decades-long program that collected brains to learn if the differences in size, shape, chemistry, or weight could account for certain behaviors or personality types (hypothesized, but never proven). At its height, the collection contained as many as 1,200 brains and parts of brains stored in glass jars preserved with formaldehyde.

The public display includes the brain of Helen Hamilton Gardener, author and prominent suffragette, who donated her brain to the collection to prove that a woman's brain was in no way inferior to a man's. Other specimens are those of six former Cornell professors, including Wilder himself, and a morbid treasure, the brain of Edward H. Rulloff, the infamous rogue known as "The Genius Killer."

Rulloff studied medicine, law, phrenology, and philology, yet he poisoned his sister-in-law and niece, killed his wife and child, and shot a furniture store clerk in Binghamton during an attempted robbery. On May 18, 1871, he was hanged for his crimes, and after an autopsy, his brain, one of the largest ever measured, came into the possession of Dr. Wilder.

His comprehensive analysis of the criminal brain was the first of its kind case study. Compared with the average male brain size of 50 ounces, Rulloff's brain weighs 59 ounces, and yes, that's even bigger than Einstein's.

Address 109 Tower Road, Cornell University, Ithaca, NY 14853, +1 (607) 255-3834, www.psychology.cornell.edu | **Getting there** From downtown Ithaca, take Route 366 (Dryden Road) to Judd Falls Road, then left onto Tower Road | **Hours** Mon–Fri 9am–4pm | **Tip** Don't miss the chance to see Cornell's most famous naked man, *Herakles in Ithaka*, a gently humorous, 11-foot-tall sculpture made of automobile bumpers by Jason Seley, dean of the University College of Architecture, standing behind Uris Hall in all his glory (109 Tower Road, Cornell University, Ithaca, NY 14853).

105 Willard Asylum

The abandoned mental hospital

Dr. Sylvester D. Willard, Surgeon General of New York, proposed a bill that would fund a humane asylum for the mentally ill, a bill that President Lincoln signed just six days before his assassination. That bill led to the building of an institution that would be named in Willard's memory.

The first patient of the Willard Asylum for the Chronic Insane was Mary Rote, who arrived on October 13, 1869. The number rapidly increased every year, as thousands more joined Mary. In 1934, the patient population reached almost 3,000. Over 50,000 patients were admitted to Willard during its years of operation, and nearly half of them died within the walls of the institution. The nearby cemetery is the final resting place of thousands of unclaimed bodies, buried in unmarked graves.

Willard was finally closed in 1995 by the New York State Office of Mental Health, and the abandoned 110-acre campus is now the stuff of nightmares. When the hospital closed, a staff member was given the task of salvaging things in all of the buildings. She unlocked an attic door in one of the buildings, where she found more than 400 suitcases, coated in dust and cobwebs, put into storage when patients were admitted to Willard and forgotten about for decades. They were filled with carefully packed belongings, often including personal mementos, letters, and items essential for daily life. It was clear that these patients held onto the expectation that their stay would be temporary, yet treatment at Willard often meant spending the remainder of their lives at the facility.

The sprawling infrastructure of the buildings that made up Willard Asylum for the Chronic Insane – a haunting reminder of the thousands of mentally ill individuals who lived and died here, and the mental health practices of a bygone era – is now enclosed with a mile-long chain fence, and access beyond the gates is prohibited.

Address Hayt Corners, Romulus, NY 14521, www.willardsuitcases.com | Getting there From Route 96A, turn onto Willard Road | Hours Unrestricted (outside the fencing) | Tip The suitcases open a small window into the lives of some of the people who lived at Willard. They were acquired by the New York State Museum in Albany and placed in a permanent collection (222 Madison Avenue, Albany, NY 12202, www.nysm.nysed.gov).

106 Willard Memorial Chapel

Tiffany's gift to the Finger Lakes

Built over two years, from 1892 to 1894, the historic Willard Chapel, one of Auburn's most cherished landmarks, was designed and crafted by the Tiffany Glass and Decorating Company of New York City. No, it wasn't Charles Tiffany, the legendary jeweler. It was his son, Louis Comfort Tiffany, better known for his work in stained glass, who created what remains as the only complete and unaltered Tiffany-designed religious interior known to exist in the world, and the last surviving complete installation by Tiffany in its original location. The project was commissioned by Caroline and Georgiana, the darling daughters of Dr. Sylvester Willard, who used their inheritances to honor their father's memory.

Patriarch of the prominent local family, Willard gave up a medical practice to manage his investments. Never mind his stocks in Chicago railroads or his acres of real estate, betting on Thomas Kingsford, a young chemist who invented a process to produce cornstarch, made Willard a fortune. Willard led a group of investors who built the Kingsford Starch Factory in Oswego, the largest producer of cornstarch in the world, and served as its president until his death.

With a healthy part of that cornstarch fortune, the two women planned what would be one of the finest examples of 19th-century architecture and design. Legend has it that Caroline and Georgiana met the younger Tiffany on a shopping trip to New York City, and impressed by his interior design of pharmaceutical millionaire George Kemp's Fifth Avenue mansion, he was given a free hand to create the entire interior of the chapel.

Visit his masterwork to see 14 opalescent windows, a rose window, a large figure window, nine Moresque-style chandeliers, memorial tablets of glass mosaic tile and gilt bronze, furnishings of oak inlaid with metal and glass mosaic, a ceiling with gold leaf stencils, and mosaic flooring.

Address 17 Nelson Street, Auburn, NY 13021, +1 (315) 252-0339, www.willard-chapel.com | **Getting there** Follow Route 34 north of center city; turn right onto Seminary Street, then left onto Nelson Street | **Hours** Wed–Sat 11am–4pm (guided tours start on the hour) | **Tip** The Willard family home, bequeathed to the Case cousins, became a research lab for Theodore Case, where he invented the process of putting sound on film, forever changing the moviegoing experience. The Cayuga Museum/Case Research Lab (203 Genesee Street, Auburn, NY 13021, www.cayugamuseum.org).

107 Willows of Seneca Lake

The shoreline's living memorials

The view of Seneca Lake from the Geneva waterfront is breathtaking and expansive. From the shore, you can see the vast stretch of the lake, its deep blue waters extending into the horizon. Seneca Lake State Park, spanning 140 scenic acres along the northern shoreline of Seneca Lake, was established in 1955, and has since become a popular destination for locals and tourists who come for a picnic spot, a place to swim, or a scenic hiking trail. For the kids, there's a playground and a sprayground with water jets that burst to life in spontaneous showers.

Safeguarding the shoreline has demanded a range of protective strategies to mitigate the relentless force of powerful winds and waves. In 1897, the existing berm on the lakeshore was raised by three feet and supported by a seawall of quarry stone, and willow trees, with their strong, extensive root systems, were planted to reduce erosion.

The graceful willow trees lining Seneca Lake not only provide protection from the elements but also stand as living memorials. Further trees were planted in the 1920s by the American Legion to honor and remember the men who died in World War I. A marker bearing the name of a fallen local soldier was originally attached to each tree, but the markers were later removed during roadside improvements.

Over the years, some of the willows have been uprooted or damaged by storms, but most remain a beloved and iconic feature of the landscape. From the park entrance, follow the loop that guides you on a leisurely drive along Park Road at the lake's edge. You'll pass hundreds of the great willows, many reaching 50 feet high and 25 feet wide, instantly recognizable with their slumping branches and dangling leaves evoking the image of tears, a natural symbol of grief. The willows of Seneca Lake lend a whisper of memory, standing as graceful witnesses to the passage of time along the shore.

Address 1 Lake Front Drive, Geneva, NY 14456, www.cityofgenevany.com | **Getting there** From Routes 5 & 20 in Geneva, turn into Park Road | **Hours** Daily 10am–6pm | **Tip** Geneva's Long Pier has served as a breakwater for the public dock area, a fishing pier, and as a recreation and tourist location. Around 1910, the pier was widened and paved with a solid surface. Take the Long Pier to "walk on the water," as it extends over 560 feet into the lake (47 Lake Front Drive, Geneva, NY 14456).

108 The Winemaker's Chapel

Miracle on Bluff Point

Paul Garrett, the son of a Confederate surgeon, founded his first winery, Garrett and Company, in North Carolina in 1900, producing the popular Virginia Dare wines, named for the first English child born in the American colonies, and the best-selling wine of its day in America. However, as the temperance movement gained momentum in the South, North Carolina became increasingly hostile to the wine industry. In response, Garrett established vineyards and wineries at several locations around the Finger Lakes region, and the Garrett family made their home among the vineyards of Bluff Point on Keuka Lake.

Despite Garrett's business success, his personal life was marked by profound tragedy. Of the seven children born to Paul and Evelyn Garrett, three daughters and four sons, all but one of the boys died in infancy, and the fourth, Charles, died of tuberculosis in 1930 at age 26. After losing Charles, the family commissioned the construction of a chapel, a sanctuary placed in the heart of their estate, nestled in the boy's favorite grove.

The Garretts were supporters of Cornell, and members of the university football team assisted in clearing the woodland slope. Designed by architect Mortimer Freehof, the chapel, perched above a breathtaking landscape, was crafted from ashlar granite, accented by cast stone decorative elements. The design includes a polygonal apse, round-arched openings, and a prominent square corner tower, crowned by a lantern and weathervane. Stained glass windows, as well as those in the crypt, were created by Frederick Wilson, the one-time head of ecclesiastical art at Tiffany Studios.

Today, after a scenic drive along Skyline Drive, past farmhouses, vineyards, and cottages on Bluff Point, you'll arrive at Garrett Chapel, barely visible in the wooded hillside. The chapel holds multi-faith services and weddings during the summer months.

Address 5251 Skyline Drive, Bluff Point, NY 14478 | Getting there From Penn Yan, take Route 54A towards Branchport; turn left on Assembly Road and right on Skyline Drive | Hours Grounds, unrestricted; interior, Jun–Sep Tue & Thu 1–4pm | Tip Bluff Point is home to Keuka Lake State Park, and a historic settlement-era burial ground containing the graves of 14 members of the Beddoe and Rose families. Follow the steep path leading from the corner of the parking area (3560 Pepper Road, Bluff Point, NY 14478, www.parks.ny.gov/parks/keukalake).

109 Wizard of Clay

Off to see the wizard

It's said that wizards live in magical enclaves, so it's not surprising to find a creative wizard in an enchanting complex of geodesic domes nestled in the hills of Bristol. Opened in 1979, the Wizard of Clay is a production workshop and retail store designed and built by pottery wizard Jim Kozlowski. And in wizard tradition, his secrets have been passed down to an apprentice, his son Jamie, who now performs his own feats of magic at the potter's wheel.

The place has a fairy-tale quality, as if it were lifted from the pages of a storybook. You're welcomed at the entrance with a sign that reads, "The Workshop Where the Wizard Works Wonders," and once inside, you're instructed to "follow the yellow brick road," bright yellow bricks painted along a path to see the wizard at work. Shelves through the first two domes are filled with an extraordinary collection of pottery, in practically every category you can think of – from pitchers, pots, pie plates, pizza stones, and piggy banks to wine goblets, toothbrush holders, sugar bowls, soup bowls, and yarn bowls, not to mention vases in all shapes, sizes, and colors.

The winding road ends in the third dome, where during most weekdays you'll see the potter at his wheel, his hands shaping mounds of clay. As the wheel spins, the once formless mass begins to rise and take shape, morphing into each vessel. Jamie uses tens of thousands of pounds of clay a year to craft as many as 17,000 functional, whimsical, and artistically inspired pieces in the ancient pottery tradition.

The Wizard of Clay's most unique items are called "Bristoleaf," objects decorated with wild plant leaves picked daily during the summer in the surrounding Bristol hills, pressed onto the soft clay. When each one is dry, it's fired in the kiln, housed in the fourth dome, and as the leaves burn off, an imprint is left in a one-of-a-kind piece.

Address 7851 Route 20A, Bloomfield, NY 14469, +1 (585) 229-2980, www.wizardofclay.com | Getting there From Canandaigua, take Route 5 & 20 west to Route 20A | Hours Daily 9am–5pm (Jan–Mar closed Thu) | Tip The Schein-Joseph International Museum of Ceramic Art at Alfred University houses nearly 8,000 ceramic and glass objects, ranging from pottery recovered from ancient civilizations to contemporary sculpture (2 Pine Street, Alfred, NY 14802, www.ceramicsmuseum.alfred.edu).

110_World's Fastest Carousel

Round and round we go!

Dr. Edwin Eldridge could not have imagined that the land he donated to the city of Elmira would evolve from a public park, growing with the community's dreams, eventually transforming into a legendary amusement park filled with thrilling rides and attractions – most notably, a historic carousel that has entertained visitors for most of a century.

Over the years, the city cleared land for a walking trail around the lake, built a picnic pavilion, restaurant, race track, small-gauge train ride through the park, several other rides, and an outdoor stage for live shows. By the 1920s, the "Golden Age" of carousels in America had arrived, and every city wanted one. In 1924, the city of Elmira placed an ad in *The New York Times* seeking a carousel for Eldridge Park, and Robert A. Long answered the ad.

Long had acquired the original Charles Looff carousel built for Atlantic City's Million Dollar Pier in 1906 after the pier replaced it with a newer version. He went on to install and manage that carousel at the park, converting 20 of the 54 carousel animals into jumpers. However, by 1988, the ride had deteriorated and the wooden animals were sold at auction.

In 2002, the Carousel Preservation Society was formed to revive one of the city's missing treasures. In an extensive renovation by members of the community, artists hand-carved and hand-painted replicas of the original animals based on vintage photographs. On May 26, 2006, the Eldridge Park carousel once again began rotating, this time with 53 newly carved horses, plus a lion, tiger, and goat. It's one of only two dozen carousels in America that still features a "ring feeder," allowing riders to attempt to "grab the brass ring" as they go round and round. The prize is a free repeat ride.

Are you ready to take a spin? As the fastest carousel in the world, it can reach speeds of approximately 18 miles per hour.

Address 96 Eldridge Park Road, Elmira, NY 14901, +1 (607) 732-8440, www.eldridgepark.org | Getting there Follow Clemens Center Parkway (Route 14) north from downtown Elmira to Eldridge Park Road | Hours Park open dawn to dusk year-round; amusement park open Jun–Sep Thu & Fri 5–9pm, Sat noon–9pm, Sun noon–8pm | Tip A visit here is the chance to see a life-sized statue that honors the memory of *American Girl*, installed in 1876, a year after the beloved mare died during a harness race at Eldridge Driving Park. Races ended in 1880, and the track was last used when Buffalo Bill brought his Wild West Show to Elmira in 1883.

111 Yellow Brick Road House

There's no place like home

While there are many interesting houses surrounding Cayuga Lake, one in particular has a tale to tell. It starts with Maud Gage, a young woman who came to Ithaca in 1880 to study at Cornell. Her roommate in the Sage Hall women's dormitory was Josie Baum, who introduced Maud to her cousin Frank Baum, member of a traveling theater troupe. The young man was smitten with Maud and promised to visit her at school.

A bit of backstory. There's a significant amount of limestone in the clays and soils of the Finger Lakes region, and when local brickworks fired these materials, the resulting color was a distinctive dull yellow hue, not the more typical orange or red. The first use of these yellow bricks in Ithaca paved a stretch of State Street, leading from downtown to the Cornell campus on East Hill.

Legend has it that when Frank arrived in Ithaca to visit Maud at Cornell, he asked for directions to the university and was told to "follow the yellow brick road." He walked along those yellow bricks as he made his way up to the East Hill campus, and it was something that obviously stuck with him.

After her sophomore year, Maud would leave Cornell, sacrificing her college education to marry Frank in 1882. Eight years later, he immortalized the "yellow brick road," a central element in his best-selling children's fairy tale, *The Wonderful Wizard of Oz*.

When Ithaca's old bricks were torn up and replaced with more-common red bricks, the yellow bricks were reused to build a house at 1114 East Shore Drive in 1939 (by coincidence, the very same year MGM's film version of *The Wizard of Oz* was released). Click your heels together and drive along the east side of Cayuga Lake. Although now a private residence and unavailable for visits, you'll be able to view that Foursquare-style, two-story house and two-car garage, all encased in the historic yellow bricks.

Address 1114 East Shore Drive (Route 34 North), Ithaca, NY 14850 | Getting there Follow State Route 13 N out of Ithaca, then take the Auburn exit to Route 34 N | Hours Viewable from the outside only | Tip For everything you ever wanted to know about Oz, visit the All Things Oz Museum (one hour away), birthplace of L. Frank Baum (219 Genesee Street, Chittenango, NY 13037, www.allthingsoz.org).

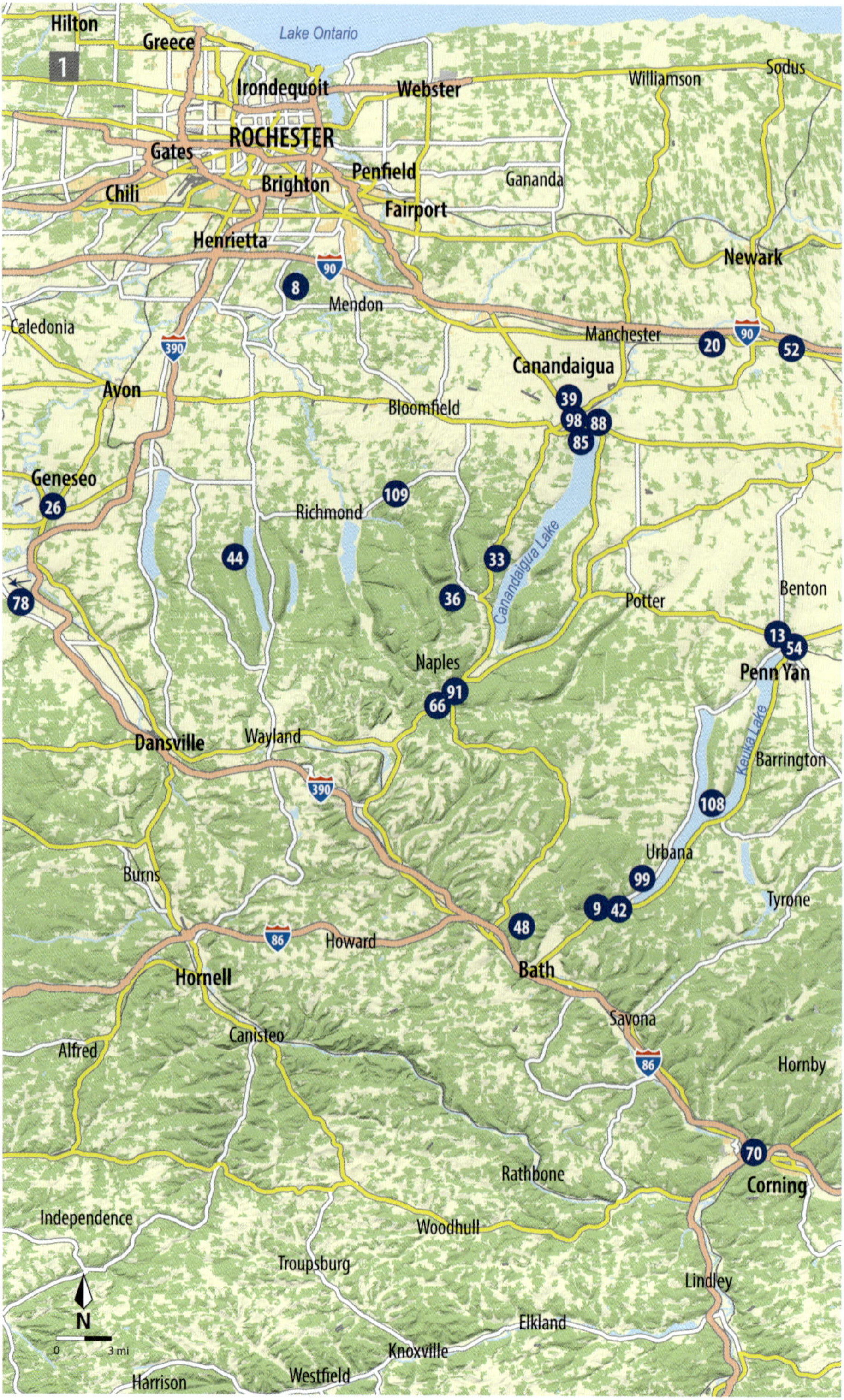
1
Lake Ontario
Hilton
Greece
Irondequoit
Webster
Williamson
Sodus
ROCHESTER
Gates
Chili
Brighton
Penfield
Fairport
Ganand
Henrietta
Newark
8
Mendon
Caledonia
Manchester
20
52
Canandaigua
Avon
Bloomfield
39
98
88
85
Geneseo
26
109
Richmond
44
33
Canandaigua Lake
78
36
Potter
Benton
13
54
Naples
Penn Yan
91
66
Dansville
Wayland
Keuka Lake
Barrington
108
Urbana
Burns
99
Tyrone
9
42
48
Howard
Hornell
Bath
Savona
Canisteo
Alfred
Hornby
70
Rathbone
Corning
Independence
Woodhull
Troupsburg
Lindley
N
Elkland
0
3 mi
Knoxville
Harrison
Westfield

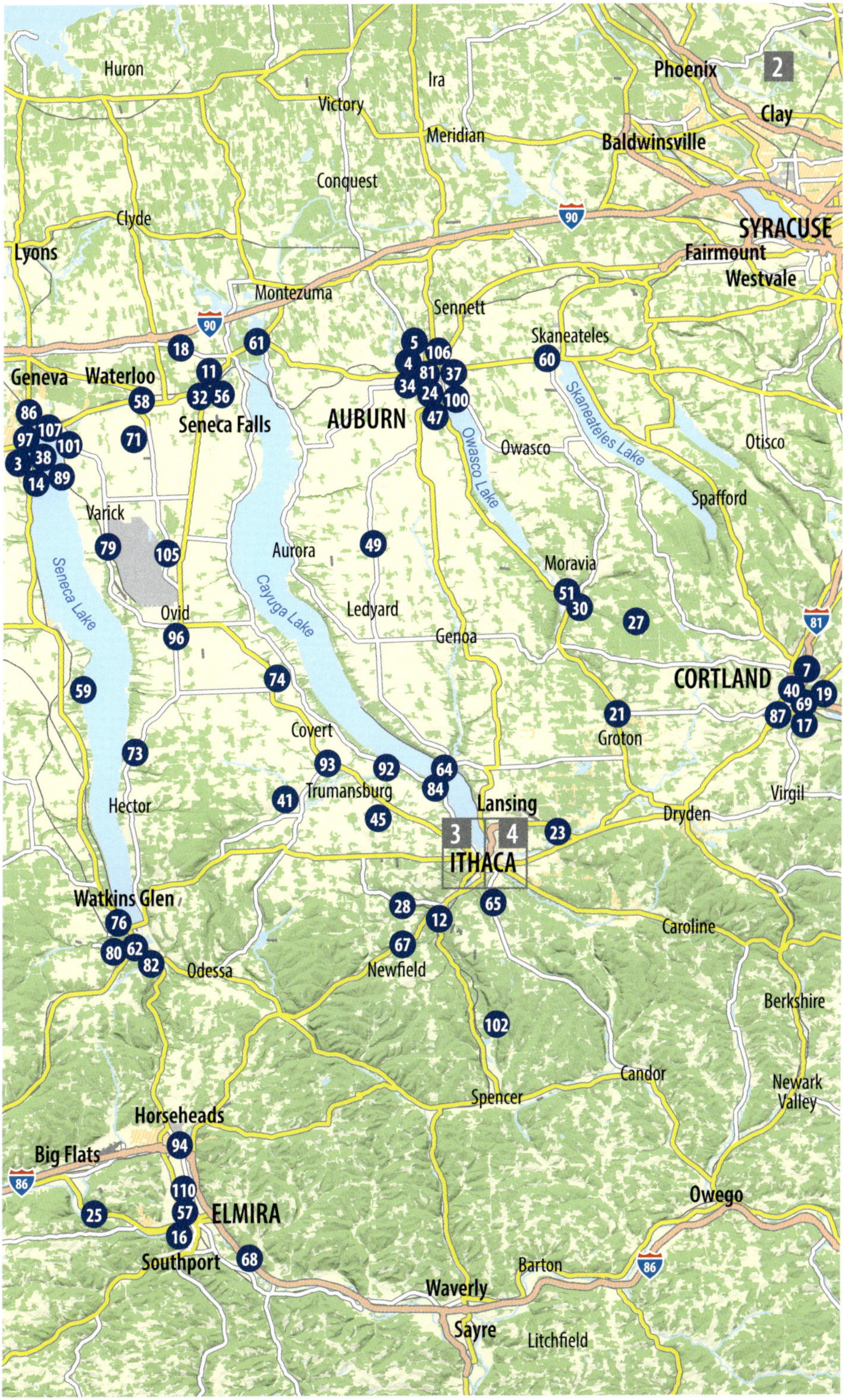

2
Huron
Ira
Phoenix
Victory
Meridian
Clay
Baldwinsville
Conquest
90
Clyde
SYRACUSE
Lyons
Fairmount
Westvale
Montezuma
Sennett
90
Skaneateles
18
61
5
106
60
Geneva
Waterloo
11
4
81
37
58
32
56
34
24
100
86
Seneca Falls
AUBURN
47
97
107
101
71
Skaneateles Lake
Owasco
Otisco
3
38
Owasco Lake
14
89
Spafford
Varick
79
105
Aurora
49
Moravia
Seneca Lake
Cayuga Lake
51
30
Ovid
Ledyard
27
96
Genoa
81
7
74
CORTLAND
59
40
19
69
21
87
17
Covert
Groton
73
93
92
64
Trumansburg
84
Virgil
Hector
41
Lansing
45
Dryden
3
4
23
ITHACA
Watkins Glen
28
65
12
Caroline
76
67
80
62
82
Odessa
Newfield
Berkshire
102
Candor
Newark Valley
Spencer
Horseheads
Big Flats
94
86
110
Owego
25
57
ELMIRA
16
Southport
68
86
Barton
Waverly
Sayre
Litchfield

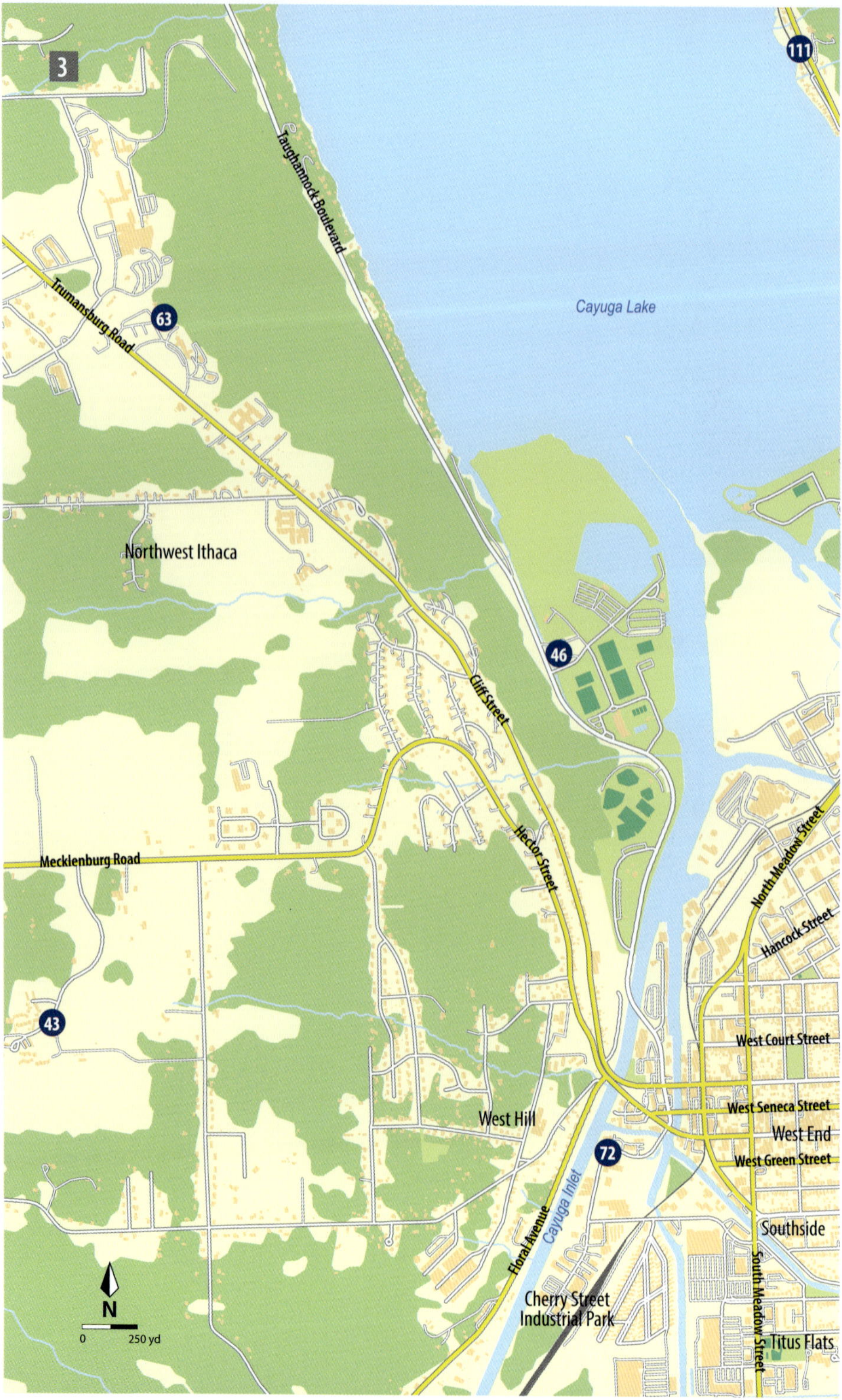

3
111
Taughannock Boulevard
Cayuga Lake
Trumansburg Road
63
Northwest Ithaca
46
Cliff Street
Hector Street
Mecklenburg Road
North Meadow Street
Hancock Street
43
West Court Street
West Seneca Street
West End
West Hill
72
West Green Street
Floral Avenue
Cayuga Inlet
Southside
South Meadow Street
Cherry Street
Industrial Park
Titus Flats
N
0
250 yd

4
North Triphammer Road
Cayuga Heights Road
Triphammer Road
Cayuga Heights
Pleasant Grove Road
103
22
Jessup Road
North Cayuga Street
Lake Street
Fall Creek
35
Thurston Avenue
Cradit Farm Drive
Judd Falls Road
Forest Home Drive
North Tioga Street
North Aurora Street
50
53
77
University Avenue
Feeney Way
2
Fall Creek
Stewart Avenue
Tower Road
104
29
Northside Triangle
6
Campus Road
Hoy Road
95
Dryden Road
1
East Buffalo Street
College Avenue
Maple Avenue
10
Downtown
Collegetown
90
75
West State Street
31
15
Cornell Street
Hudson Street
South Plain Street
South Albany Street
ITHACA
East State Street
Mitchell Street
83
55
Six Mile Creek
Giles Street

Jo-Anne Elikann, Susan Lusk
111 Places in New York That You Must Not Miss
ISBN 978-3-7408-2400-6

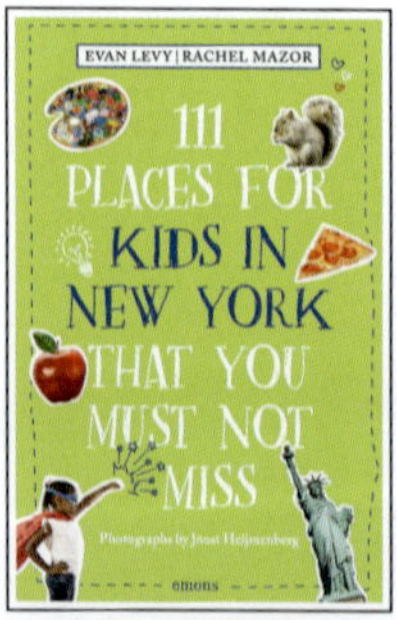

Evan Levy, Rachel Mazor, Joost Heijmenberg
111 Places for Kids in New York That You Must Not Miss
ISBN 978-3-7408-1993-4

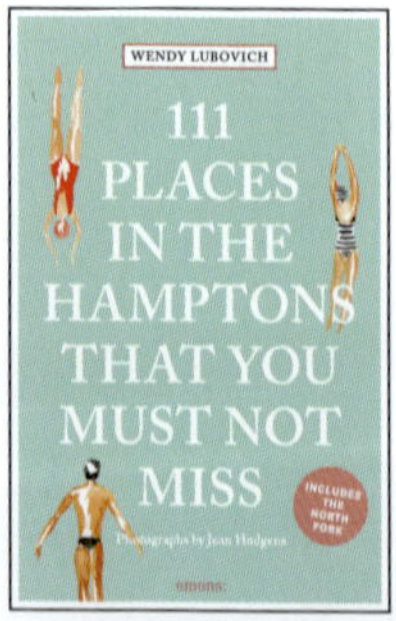

Wendy Lubovich, Jean Hodgens
111 Places in the Hamptons That You Must Not Miss
ISBN 978-3-7408-2570-6

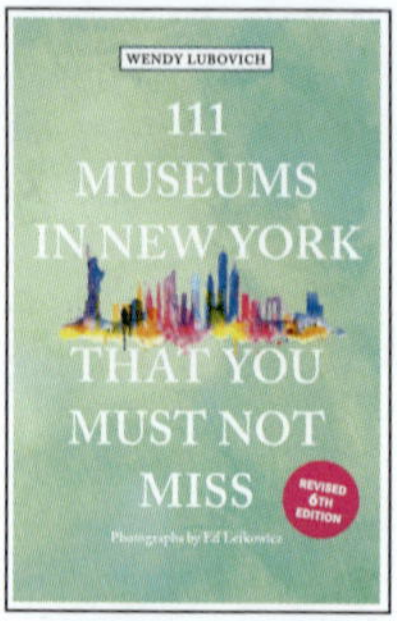

Wendy Lubovich, Ed Lefkowicz
111 Museums in New York That You Must Not Miss
ISBN 978-3-7408-2374-0

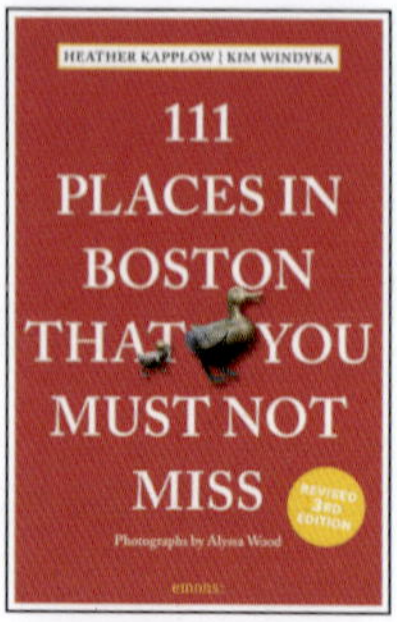

Kim Windyka, Heather Kapplow, Alyssa Wood
111 Places in Boston That You Must Not Miss
ISBN 978-3-7408-2655-0

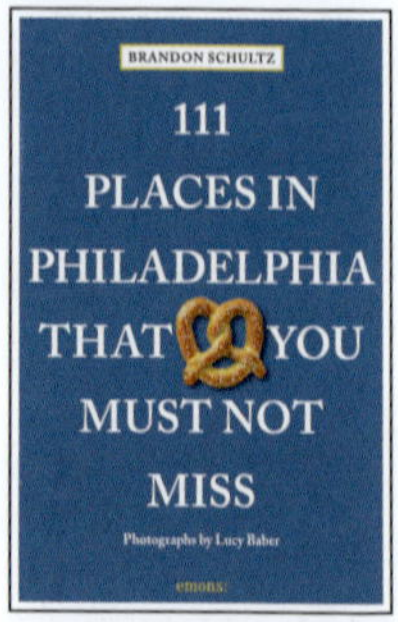

Brandon Schultz, Lucy Baber
111 Places in Philadelphia That You Must Not Miss
ISBN 978-3-7408-1376-5

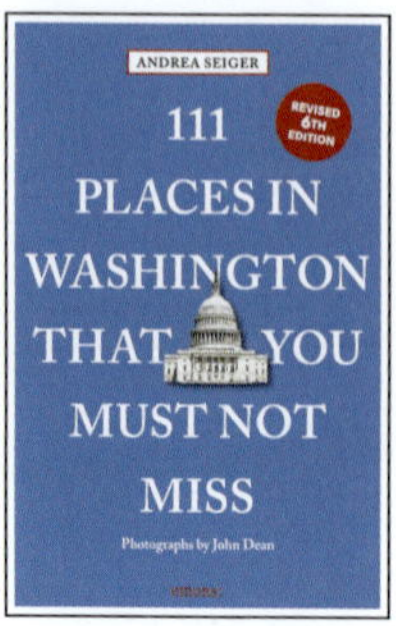

Andrea Seiger, John Dean
111 Places in Washington That You Must Not Miss
ISBN 978-3-7408-2656-7

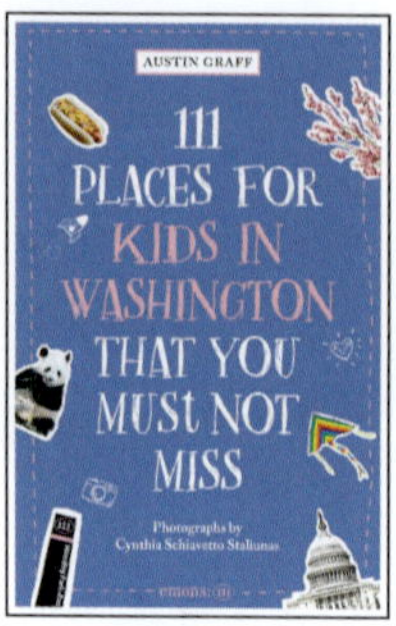

Austin K. Graff, Cynthia Schiavetto Staliunas
111 Places for Kids in Washington, DC That You Must Not Miss
ISBN 978-3-7408-2428-0

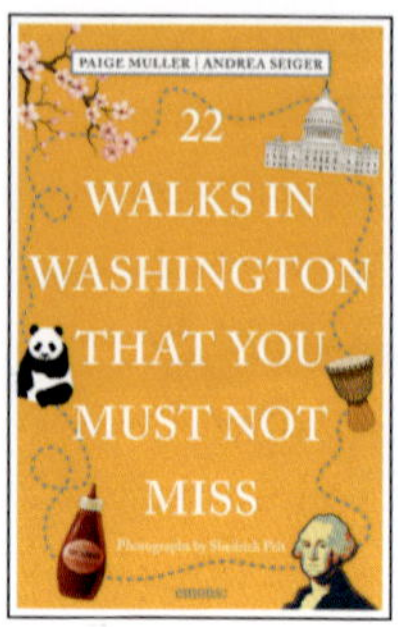

Andrea Seiger, Paige Mulle, Shedrick Pelt
22 Walks in Washington, DC That You Must Not Miss
ISBN 978-3-7408-1987-3

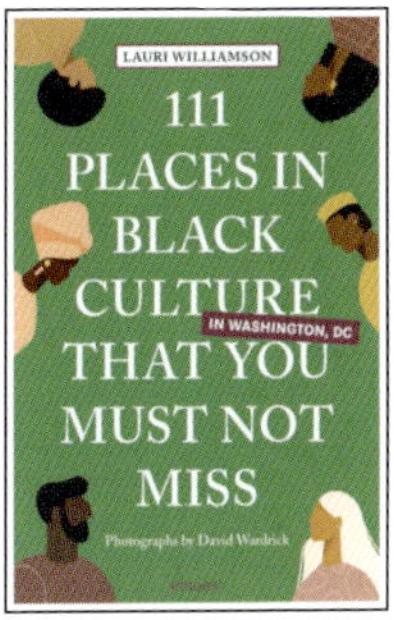

Lauri Williamson, David Wardrick
111 Places in Black Culture in Washington, DC That You Must Not Miss
ISBN 978-3-7408-2003-9

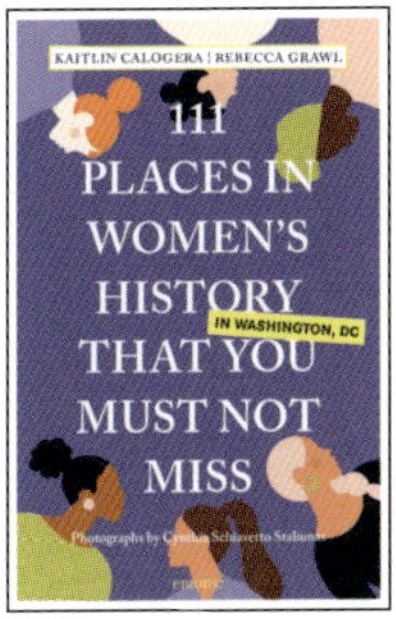

Kaitlin Calogera, Rebecca Grawl, Cynthia Schiavetto Staliunas
111 Places in Women's History in Washington That You Must Not Miss
ISBN 978-3-7408-1590-5

John Tucker, Ashley Tucker
111 Places in Richmond That You Must Not Miss
ISBN 978-3-7408-2653-6

Amy Bizzarri, Susie Inverso
111 Places in Chicago That You Must Not Miss
ISBN 978-3-7408-2402-0

Dana DuTerroil, Joni Fincham, Daniel Jackson
111 Places in Houston That You Must Not Miss
ISBN 978-3-7408-2265-1

Dana DuTerroil, Joni Fincham, Sara S. Murphy
111 Places for Kids in Houston That You Must Not Miss
ISBN 978-3-7408-2267-5

Kelsey Roslin, Nic Yeager, Jesse Pitzler
111 Places in Austin That You Must Not Miss
ISBN 978-3-7408-1642-1

Travis Swann Taylor
111 Places in Atlanta That You Must Not Miss
ISBN 978-3-7408-1887-6

Gordon Streisand, Alex Streisand
111 Places in Miami and the Keys That You Must Not Miss
ISBN 978-3-7408-2403-7

Susan Veness,
Simon Veness, Kayla Smith
111 Places in Orlando That You Must Not Miss
ISBN 978-3-7408-1900-2

Cristyle Egitto, Jakob Takos
111 Places in Palm Beach That You Must Not Miss
ISBN 978-3-7408-2398-6

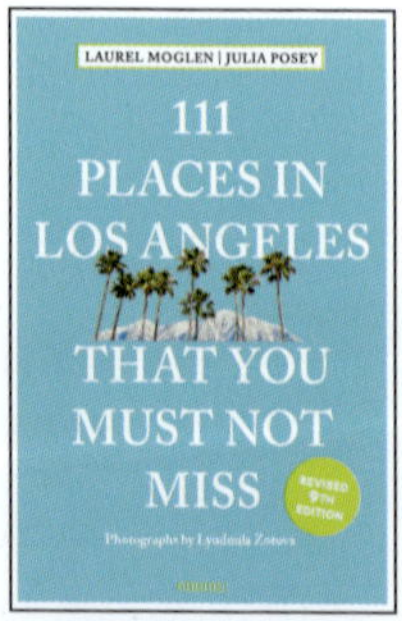

Laurel Moglen, Julia Posey,
Lyudmila Zotova
111 Places in Los Angeles That You Must Not Miss
ISBN 978-3-7408-2573-7

Stephanie Arsenault
111 Places in San Diego That You Must Not Miss
ISBN 978-3-7408-1540-0

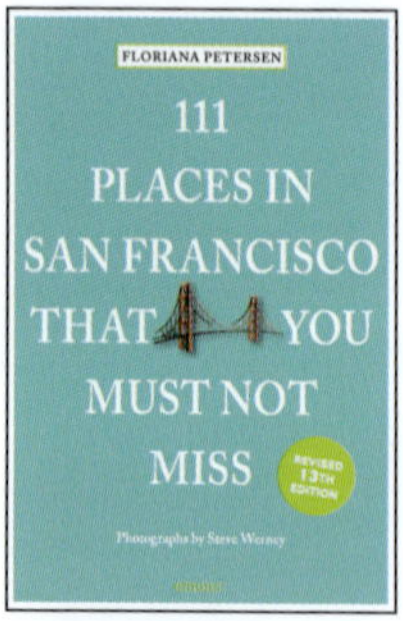

Floriana Petersen,
Steve Werney
111 Places in San Francisco That You Must Not Miss
ISBN 978-3-7408-2882-0

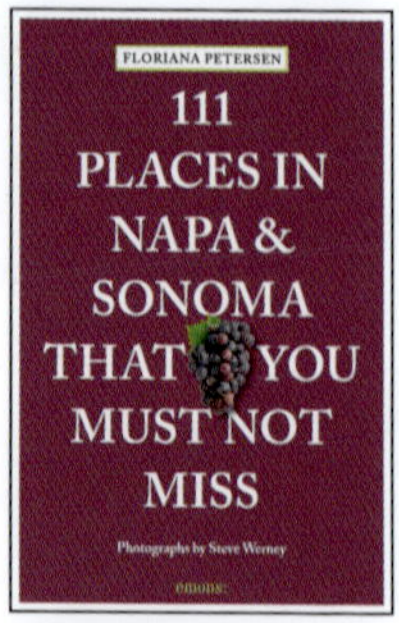

Floriana Petersen,
Steve Werney
111 Places in Napa and Sonoma That You Must Not Miss
ISBN 978-3-7408-1553-0

Harriet Baskas, Cortney Kelley
111 Places in Seattle That You Must Not Miss
ISBN 978-3-7408-2375-7

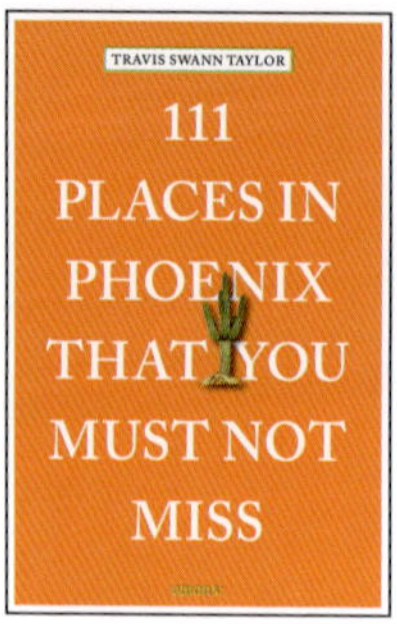

Travis Swann Taylor
111 Places in Phoenix That You Must Not Miss
ISBN 978-3-7408-2050-3

Philip D. Armour, Susie Inverso
111 Places in Denver That You Must Not Miss
ISBN 978-3-7408-1220-1

Acknowledgements

Every book begins with someone who believes in it first. For me, that someone was Dennis Hayes. Over the years, Dennis has introduced me to more projects than I can count, each one a new adventure. This time, he made the case that I should be the one to tell the stories of these places, and for his encouragement, I am profoundly grateful.

To Karen Seiger and Laura Olk of Emons Verlag, who guided me along the journey. To Ros Horton, my editor, who kept these pages clear and true, and Karolin Meinert, whose design elevated the book's presentation. It's a privilege to be part of the *111 Places* series.

And finally, to some of the folks I met along the way: Anthony Pacini, Andre Wigley, Ernie Warren, Kip Zeiter, Alison Chapin, Lynn White, Joseph Inverso, Sarah Byers and Lynne Doyle, Vicki Danahy, Jay Dutcher, Drew Clare, Stephen Lewandowski and Marita Wallace, Terry Stewart and Bill Holgate, Trudy Buxenbaum and Marilyn Post, Jackie Bakker, Michael Porter, Gerry Collins, Frank Arpino, Kristin Welch, Megan Robinson, Robert Norton, Will King, Rob Garrison, Sophie Clough, Kirk House, Korey Buzzell, Jamie Bashford and Chief Patrick Elwell, Mark and Lynette Wood, Ngawang Dhondup, Jordan Governale, Deirdre Stafford Stevenson, Richard Malcolm, Frédéric Bouché, John Tamburello, Bee Parisi, Emma Dailey, Wayne Myers, Brett Brubaker, Graham Ottoson, Kyle Kubick, Rita Edwards, Jim Kozlowski, Alfred Ritz, Deborah Denome, Scott Oldfield, Leslyn McBean-Clairborne, Cydney Wixon, Claire Dehm, Doreen Culver-Foss, and Annemarie Zwack. They often interrupted busy lives to share a story, a memory, or simply a laugh. Their generosity gave this book its voice.

Michael Turback is a former restaurateur and saloonkeeper. After studies at Cornell University, he created one of Upstate New York's first destination restaurants, pioneering farm-to-table, vineyard-to-glass, and craft cocktail movements. *The Los Angeles Times* called Turback's of Ithaca "the first Finger Lakes restaurant to really devote itself to New York's culinary and enological bounty." Michael has journeyed through every corner of the region, and this book, part of a wide-ranging body of work, best reflects his lifelong passion for travel, discovery, and storytelling. www.michaelturback.com

Brian Wilder is a seasoned freelance photographer specializing in advertising, editorial, and corporate work. His visual style and sharp storytelling have earned him the trust of major clients, including AT&T, IKEA, This Old House, Timberland, Titleist, and Volkswagen. He has served as in-house photographer for both Kodak and Fisher-Price and has taught Advertising Photography at the Rochester Institute of Technology. Notable assignments have taken him behind the scenes at the Academy Awards, the People's Choice Awards, as well as on tour with the PGA. www.bwilder.com